The Search for the Real Earle

A Journey into the Self

by Earle G. Harris

Teresa,
What a joy to have you in my life. I will miss you very much. Hope we can stay in touch.
Love,
Earle

EARLE G. HARRIS

THE SEARCH FOR THE REAL EARLE

A Journey into the Self

The author will donate any profits of the sale of this book to charitable organizations, including any stipends received from promoting the message in this book.

Preface

" ... The Saints of all major religions answer with one voice: while we can draw inspiration from those who practice love in their daily lives we all have the syllabus of love right inside us, printed on every cell. We need to look no further afield. There burns in the recesses of our consciousness a divine spark of pure love, universal, unquenchable. No matter what difficulties we manage to get ourselves and others into in our ignorance, whatever the country we live in, or the race we belong to, whether we are rich or poor, learned or ignorant, this spark is never extinguished. *It is our greatest glory.*

"Then the Saints go even further. They tell that life has only one overriding purpose: to discover this source, to discover the source of infinite love."

— *Climbing the Blue Mountain* by Eknath Easwaran
Blue Mountain Center of Meditation, Tomales, California

> He is forever free who has broken
> Out of the ego-cage of *I* and *mine*
> To be united with the Lord of Love.
> This is the supreme state. Attain this
> And pass from death to immortality.

— *Bhagavad Gita*
Indian Scripture

Foreword

What we have here, in *The Search for the Real Earle,* is a spiritual autobiography of an extraordinary man. Reading it, I find myself sensing the true nature of this man, and this, I must say, is an exhilarating and healing experience.

Not that I am surprised. It's been my pleasure and privilege to know Earle Harris for many years, to work alongside him in countless ways. And I can tell you from much first-hand experience, this is a rare and special person. He really lives the love he speaks about. He's the real thing. He is a beacon of light and hope to all who know him.

Earle is a very pure being. He's so pure, in fact, that some of what he says may at first strike some of us as simplistic. That's because we are accustomed to look to books for excitement, complexity, and mental stimulation, for drama and entertainment. But reading *The Search for the Real Earle* is not like reading the hard-hitting action-packed sizzling blockbusters the book industry continually produces. It doesn't jump up and down demanding attention. It doesn't wear us out trying to be glamorous or exotic. It doesn't leave us feeling excited, jaded and exhausted, like so much of contemporary society. Instead, reading *The Search for the Real Earle* is like taking a walk in a beautiful forest with a deep and trusted friend – and discovering a gorgeous babbling brook whose soft murmurs speak to your heart like the music of God. It's a soulful book that leaves us feeling rested, whole, and free.

Sometimes, in my darker moments, I've wondered why God ever created our species the way he has. Seeing so much of the destruction human beings have visited upon each other and the rest of Creation, I've had moments of being ashamed of being human. But knowing Earle has made those moments less frequent and less frightening. He has made me feel far better about being a human being. One thing I know for sure: the God that created Earle Harris is a loving God. The Universe that has produced an Earle Harris is a Universe for which I want to belong. This man helps me honor my path. He makes me glad to be alive.

I'm so very grateful I've gotten to know Earle in my lifetime. He is a fine and pure and dear soul. Let his soft voice be as nectar for your spirit, as it has for mine.

— *John Robbins*

The Search for the Real Earle
A Journey into the Self

The Search for the Real Earle.
Copyright © 1998 by Earle G. Harris.
Excerpts may be used or reprinted with
credit given to the author. Larger use or
reprints must be approved by the author.

First publication October 1998,
by True Heart Publishers, PO Box 2174,
Santa Cruz, California 95063

ISBN: 0-9666965-0-6

This book has been printed on recycled
paper with non-toxic ink. ♻

Acknowledgments

John Robbins, author of *Diet for a New America*, for his love, inspiration, and message that have changed the lives of millions, including mine.

Deo Robbins, a dear friend who is always near with her love and gentleness.

Ocean and Michelle Robbins, through their youth and love have kept me young in both age and heart.

John and Marilyn Crisler, who have supported me through 25 rough years in my search for the real Earle.

My son Keith, who has accepted my weirdness and has been a sounding board for a lot of my craziness. I have gained much from his knowledge and our diversity.

My daughter Kathy for continuing to love me as my life has gradually changed from that of social robot to a free spirit. She is a real joy in my life.

Patricia Carney for her loving friendship and for gently nudging me into being more caring and accepting of myself.

Shams and Amanda Kairys who have been instrumental on my spiritual journey.

Mary, Frank, and Koa who have shared my life and journey and added joy to both.

Eleanor Wasson, my dear friend and mentor whose wisdom continues to guide me toward another world – and back.

Ian and Terry Thiermann who have made my search full of joy and laughter.

The Board of Directors of EarthSave International whose lives, both individually and collectively, have influenced me through their leadership, common bond, compassion, conflict resolution, and expertise in directing EarthSave activities.

My family of EarthSave staff and volunteers whose love, respect, and honor have added joy to my journey.

All those thousands of individuals who have influenced my life, either personally or through books and cassette tapes. To mention only a few; Ram Dass, Wayne Dyer, Leo Buscaglia, Eknath Easwaran, Larry Dossey, Deepak Chopra, Thomas Berry, Nathaniel Branden, and Denis Waitley.

And to all the Angels both in heaven and on earth who have guided my life and spirit in paths unknown to me, even when I thought I knew best.

My deep appreciation to the following persons who have contributed to the successful publishing of this book.

Steve Lustgarden, for unscrambling my atrocious grammar and writing skills into a readable manuscript.

To Eleanor Wasson, John Robbins, Patricia Carney, and Ed Fieberg for their review, comments, and loving support during my long process in making my dream come true.

To Rich Curtis, for the design and production of the book.

And to *Publishers Press* of Salt Lake City, Utah for printing.

Table Of Contents

- iii   Title Page
- v   Preface
- vi   Foreword
- ix   Acknowledgments

- 1   The Search Begins
- 8   A New Career Begins
- 11   The Simple Life
- 18   Awareness
- 24   Communication With All Life
- 30   Two Magnificent Universes
- 36   Meditation
- 46   Life On The Road / with photographs
- 54   Nature As My Teacher
- 57   From All - I Have Learned
- 61   Acceptance
- 65   Responsible Service
- 69   The Elusive Soul
- 73   Soul Mates
- 78   EGO-Mania
- 82   World Citizen
- 87   A World in Crisis
- 92   United Nations
- 97   World Hunger
- 101   Aging and Death
- 107   The Future Search
- 109   How to Contact the Author

XII *The Search for the Real Earle*

The Search Begins

In 1970 I believed I was a model citizen. I had a degree in engineering and a career with NASA in the Space Program. I was married with two grown children and involved in many community activities. I looked forward to an early retirement and was studying to become a minister in the Methodist Church.

But something inside me was very disturbed. I seemed to be trapped in a lifestyle that was not in line with my true self and the service that I felt called to perform. I was becoming disenchanted with the organized church as it did not satisfy my spiritual needs. I struggled with the conflicts within and the controls from without which eventually resulted in a divorce and my withdrawing from the organized church.

It was a choice that was unacceptable in our society at that time, but I felt God was smiling on me as I chose the freedom to follow my dreams. There were many difficult years to follow as I struggled to free myself from much of the past but I accepted the challenge to find the real Earle. Since then I have been searching for this elusive bundle of energy called Earle, and the path that might lead me to infinite love.

How was I to begin and what price was I willing to pay?

2 The Search for the Real Earle

This book gives some insight into how I met the challenge and freed myself of many of the chains that had been neatly woven into a massive fence around me since I came into this world on July 18, 1924. My story began long before I made that conscious choice to seek my own path.

Once there was a *real Earle*. I was born, given a name, and then, as happens to most of us, the great cover up of who we really are began. Every segment of our society played a part in this conspiracy. First, it was my parents, then the schools, then organized religion – followed by other authority figures, all molding me into their model of a "good citizen". The real *self* was lost in a maze. On those occasions when I tried to reverse the trend I would find myself disciplined until the urge finally disappeared, the battle too great. By the time I had reached voting age I had become a "social robot" – a *solid citizen* and a leader in the community! I must remind you that no one was deliberately involved in this cover up; everyone was just doing what was socially expected and divinely correct!

In the beginning … I was born from the miraculous union between a sperm and an egg. But was this really the beginning? Are we limited by our present knowledge and concepts passed down through the generations? It is true that we became form, a physical entity – the one we can touch, feel, see, hear, and smell through our five senses, at what we refer to as birth. Is that who we really are? Could it be that there is another dimension that is more than we dare to unveil?

Where was this *real Earle* hiding? When did this miracle really begin? Was it at birth, at conception, or eons before? How far back would I have to search? At one time I believed the beginning was at my physical birth but the more I have searched and the more I have learned about the connection of all life, the more confused I have become as to when my life really began. I now believe that life abounds throughout the universe and I am a product of all history. Therefore my pilgrimage must have begun before I became a physical form. Hopefully, my pilgrimage will end as it began – as a bundle of energy connected to the universal spirit, God.

Growing up in the south during the depression years was a blessing in disguise. It was a time without luxuries, and in many cases without the bare essentials. My father worked with the post office and was fortunate to have a steady job during those years. Most people lived in rural areas where they knew little of what was happening outside their own community. Most of the men worked in FDR's federal programs which built many of our National Parks and such projects as the Hoover Dam. I was born in a small community called Flat Rock, Tennessee which later became part of Nashville. Ours was a simple life devoid of all the luxuries of today. I recall the days when a weekend trip was to travel to Columbia, my dad's old homestead 40 miles away, in our model A Ford, and ride tractors around the farm.

I belonged to the Boy Scouts, played neighborhood sports, had a cold drink stand in my front yard, sold fireworks at Christmas time, and played in my father's five piece family band (ugh) at PTA meetings and other local activities. As I grew older, band became my greatest thrill during high school as we played at all the sports events, and I belonged to the Sons of the American Legion Drum and Bugle Corps. These activities seem very mundane today but mine was a life of joy at the time.

My ambition all through school was to join the Navy and see the world aboard ship. I got my wish. As I graduated, World War II began and I hastened off to the recruiting office to sign up and go fight the enemy. Little did I know what lay in store for me. I did get to see all the Pacific Islands but they weren't the ports I had envisioned. After the war I was fortunate to get a college degree at the government's expense. Soon thereafter, I joined the Space Program which was just becoming a serious science in this country.

During a 35 year career with NASA I was fortunate to have played a part in some of humanity's greatest endeavors and achievements, including the early satellite projects, the Apollo moon shots, the Skylab project, and the Shuttle missions. I joined the Space Program when von Braun and his team of 120 German scientists were transferred to Huntsville, Alabama after World War II. I was a recent engineering graduate with no knowledge of rocketry at all. It was a great experience to associate with such esteemed scientists and enter into a wonderful career which has taken us on a marvelous adventure into space.

During the Apollo missions photos were sent back to earth of this magnificent blue planet on which we live. As I viewed these photos a transformation gradually emerged within me with a deeper appreciation and concern for all life on this planet. I began to question the rationale of our technology in relationship with many of the social ills facing us. Could we effectively divide or integrate our priorities to serve both? In the early 70s, very few understood the devastation we were creating for our lives and for our planet. My life went through drastic changes, both materially and spiritually. By the time I retired in 1985 my emphasis had shifted from technology to personal growth and social needs.

When I first began my search I had no idea of the depth it would take. The first step was to free myself of the bonds others had tightly placed on my life and find my own uniqueness in response. Also, I had to begin living in a positive world, not the negative world to which I was accustomed, and find my own spiritual path. I was born and raised in the very conservative deep south at a time when the Puritan and Victorian themes were the underlying truth of the society. Also the Christian approach was the prime source for my religious training. How dare I question all of my early teachings and venture into the vast unknown in search of the *real Earle*. There were so many things I did not like about myself that I almost gave up the search before it even started.

During my career with NASA I had learned about the magnificent universe that surrounds our own planet, but I was becoming more aware of the magnificent universe within my own body. So, over time my interest moved toward my own health and this fabulous physical body we call home. As my search continued it was to find out who was this individual hiding beneath the surface. It was through personal growth of this human body, I decided, that would allow me to be a better servant during my travels on this planet. To my amazement, the further I searched, the more my trek became a spiritual journey in search of that infinite universal love where all things become one.

Thus, the path that started as an ego trip was now two. One is the magnificent physical form in which most of our daily lives are concerned. The other is the spiritual aspect that occupies no physical space, is not seen, and has no weight. The more we are in touch with our spirit the less we are engrossed with the ego. My goal was to move toward the transition from the ego to the spiritual state where I might come in contact with the *real Earle* and with God.

As I reach this plateau in my search I marvel at the process that has taken place in my life. I am overwhelmed at the changes; the deeper awareness of spirit, the depth of communication with all life, the acceptance of things as they are, a more intense form of meditation, a more simple life, becoming a world citizen, and a deeper love for all things. As I recognize that life is only a process, I am excited about what lies ahead for me and wonder what my involvement will be.

My hope is that my personal experience will motivate you to pick up the pace of your own search. There is a special and unique you different from all others and if you don't live and tell your own story, that uniqueness will be lost for all time. Your search will no doubt take different paths from mine but your openness and meditative practice will guide you toward our mutual goal of infinite love.

I know my search for the *real Earle* will not end during this lifetime; however, this is one person's approach into the search for himself over the past 25 years. The deeper I search, the deeper meaning I find both spiritually and in the service I provide; in fact, they become more one and the same. So join me as we share this journey while I search for me and you search for you, where our paths may cross many times and where our enlightenment will encompass all life on this earth and the far reaches of the universe.

One last observation. If your heart is touched by the contents of this book it probably won't be from my years growing up during the depression, my years in the Navy during World War II, my career with NASA, or my years helping to save this planet. It will no doubt be those moments that were written through my tears, both pain and joy, and the deep emotional issues dealing with my spiritual pilgrimage, for that is where the true heart is. Many times as I am listening to tapes or while reading books, or just listening to someone's personal story, something will touch my soul and tears will run down my face. It has struck a chord within me at the heart level. My hope is that parts of this book may strike you in the same way and that you too may identify within yourself some of these experiences.

A New Career Begins

My heart was pounding at the beauty of the sunrise reflecting on the great Pacific Ocean as I stood beneath the lighthouse on the beach at Santa Cruz, California. The year was 1990. My first thoughts carried me back half a century when I had set sail across the mighty Pacific into the Big War. This time, however, my arrival on the west coast marked a different mission, maybe a mission of equal importance. Once again, I felt called to stand on the front line, but this time to join in the struggle to save our planet, to help make it a healthier place for all humankind, and to live in peace with one another and with nature.

How did this Alabama boy end up in California? As my space career ended in 1985 I sought new paths for my journey. After several years of teaching and encouraging others to examine their own lives, I read a book by John Robbins entitled *Diet for a New America*. The book changed my life. Even though my life was already experiencing profound change, *Diet for a New America* added a new dimension to be considered. I had been a vegetarian for many years and was also quite concerned about the environment, but *Diet for a New America* radically altered how I think about food and agriculture. It opened my eyes

A winner is born

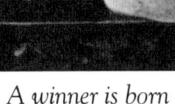

The style of the twenties, author in front

like never before to the depth of suffering that farm animals today endure, from birth to slaughter. And it awakened me to the pantheon of human diseases that are inextricably tied to what we place on the ends of our forks, especially the meat and dairy products. *Diet for a New America* shook me to my very foundation.

Six months later, motivated by this new knowledge and awareness, I sold my home, disposed of all my material possessions, and, hardest of all, severed 40 years of Alabama roots and emotional ties, and headed west. My goal was to join the staff of EarthSave International, the organization spawned to respond to the uprising of popular support and concern triggered by *Diet for a New America*. I wished to help people understand how the eating habits of the standard American family are impacting human health, the land, water, and air. My cross-country journey was exciting and thoughtful as I contemplated how these dramatic changes would influence my inner search.

So, as I turned from the awe and beauty of the sunrise over Monterey Bay, and with great excitement and energy, and a full heart of expectations, I opened the door to EarthSave and a new phase of my journey. My new career and home far exceeded my expectations. I was made to feel like one of the family that very first day. Of course, I brought with me my Alabama drawl that charmed my new California friends.

Santa Cruz is a small beach town of 50,000 or so, except on weekends and during the summer when people flood over the Santa Cruz mountains from San Jose, San Francisco, Oakland and beyond to enjoy the region's beautiful beaches and redwood forests. Santa Cruz also sports a very alluring leisurely and progressive pace and quality of life, that I found wonderful. This lifestyle, in combination with the area's unparalleled natural beauty, provided the ideal setting for the continuation of my personal quest. What I had only dreamed and read about for 20 years was finally coming more into focus; an opportunity to reach deeper into my soul and get a closer look at the *real Earle* hiding there.

The Simple Life

When I started in search of the *real Earle* I realized something that I had known as a boy but lost sight of after the war - that I am best suited for a simple life. My life today is as it was during my growing-up years, with few material possessions. This allows me to place value on the things that are most important to me – service, nature, and spiritual growth. As a boy my material deprivation was simply the way it was. Today it is by choice.

As stated earlier, growing up in the South during the depression turned out to be a great blessing for me. It was an opportunity to live a very simple life – not necessarily one of choice – but we didn't know that we weren't rich. For many it was a life without luxuries and in many cases, without even bare essentials. Can you imagine a life with no TV, no computers, no electrical appliances, a model-T Ford for transportation, and no running water with outhouses for bathrooms? Sounds a lot like a Third World country, doesn't it? I know you have heard this story many times from some elder in your family, so I won't belabor the point except to say that we generally don't miss what we don't have, especially if it doesn't exist. But once we have or know of such luxuries, today we often feel deprived without them.

Something I didn't realize in my youth was that I was born a very frugal person. Not only did I grow up in a simple environment but my genes were in total agreement. All through the years before World War II I was happy with the simple things; I never coveted things that I didn't have, or that others had. This enhanced my chances of having a happy childhood, not resenting others if they had more than I did. So this laid a foundation for me not to desire the material things in life. But something went amiss. My genetic predisposition towards frugality was derailed.

After the war there came a time of plenty. Having been in the service I had the opportunity to get a college education at the government's expense. Then there was marriage with two children at a time when *things* became a way of life. New cars, new homes, nice clothes, plus the desire to give my kids everything I didn't have in my youth. So, I got caught up in the rat race. Having a career with the government didn't allow me to have many of the things that others had, but it was a good life. Each house and each car was a little larger and more expensive than the one before. I am not ashamed that I gave my family an opportunity to live a more comfortable life, but for myself, I could have accepted a simpler life than the times permitted.

One of the big rewards of living a simple life is that I'm free of all the responsibilities that go along with ownership. As I began to devote less time and value to material things, I found that I had less stress and more free time, time which I could use serving others and staying in touch with nature. Most of us readily admit that material possessions are not the most important thing in our lives yet our actions don't support this.

Living a simple lifestyle is fundamental to me and my

happiness. Whatever formulated this view was surely established early in my life. All through my youth things were not important to me – not only because I had very few material things, but something deep inside me said they weren't important.

As I grew older this viewpoint was supported by other teachings. Later, my view of Christ's simple lifestyle emphasized my view of material things. Today, I still believe that it is harder for a rich man to enter the kingdom of heaven than it is for a camel to go through the eye of a needle. And when the rich man asked what he was to do to be saved, Jesus told him, "go sell all you have and give the money to the poor, then come follow me." Sadly, the rich man turned away. All of the Spiritual leaders and Saints that I have studied to date have lived very simple lives. I wonder how I can improve on the wisdom of such greatness. I still have the idea that the "love of money is the root of all evil". I still have the view that most of our world's problems can be directly attributed to our unsatiable desire for material wealth.

The biggest advantage I have in living a simple life is that I have a nice retirement check coming each month and health insurance for life. Financially I am secure and as long as the government shall stand I am well provided for. So how do I justify asking others to consider a simple lifestyle when they may not have the security that I have? When I retired in 1985 I made a commitment that I would always have a zero balance in my checkbook at the beginning of each month, so what is left always goes to some charitable need. Further, I vowed to myself that I would never again accept monetary or material value for services performed. My retirement check is quite capable of meeting all my financial needs and I don't want the heavy burden of financial management. I feel that I can live my chosen lifestyle considerably below the poverty level and not far above the so called "street people" needs. God has blessed me in so many ways and the value I place on my life has nothing to do with financial or material values but only the service I can provide for others and the spiritual love I experience through the deep reverence I share with the Universe and with God.

With this background you may better understand why, in later years, I have been able to revert to my childhood views about living a very simple life. I feel that many of us – generally as we get older – recognize that the real value of life is not in material possessions but we fail in our transition to a more purposeful life as our security and dependence on luxuries are deeply embedded. As my needs continue to simplify, I am free to live my life without dependency on social responsibilities and social mores – and to be more in balance with the universe.

At one time I thought the theme of this book would be "voluntary simplicity" but as I assessed the total message, there is a lot more to my search than only living a simple life. Also, a great book already exists entitled *Voluntary Simplicity* by Duane Elgin, which is worthy of your review. As my life becomes more and more world-oriented and I see the immensity of its poverty and ill health, how can I justify a lifestyle of luxury and say that it is part of God's plan?

I surely try not to impose my simplicity on others, but I have seen too many of the ills of our society caused by greed for money and material things. And the time consumed by our attention to these matters is enormous.

Many years ago I kept records for a seven month period to determine how much of my time was spent maintaining all the things I owned. I was shocked to find that I spent 35 percent of my time taking care of my possessions. Even more important is what has happened to me spiritually. It opened up more heavenly doors for me in my search for the *real Earle*.

So, as a result of my beliefs, I continue to search for simpler ways to live. I have gradually disposed of most of my material possessions; however, I have some things stored that I'm still hanging on to. I can't let loose of my personal contact with the past, of so many warm and beautiful memories. The only things I own of any material value are my 1990 van that I use in my travels around the country and my little PowerBook computer that keeps me in touch with the world. When I bought my van three years ago the odometer registered 100,000 miles. I could have afforded a newer one, especially as it is also my home, but I felt better options for a more frugal approach.

Even though I choose to live a very simple life it must be strongly said that I have no desire to become part of a monastery. I have no problem with those who choose that way of life but I am a very social and service-oriented person who keeps in contact with the world. As I discuss in a later chapter, I consider myself a world citizen and desire to serve all life on this globe.

When I go into a town one of the first things I locate are the thrift stores and the flea markets. Most of my needs can be satisfied there and the simple task of recycling fills my heart with joy. When I think of our landfills being filled with used "stuff" I know I don't need to contribute to that nightmare. Our planet is becoming a junkyard because today, in our land of plenty, it is more economical to buy new things than to repair. It breaks my heart to see the horrible conditions in much of the world as we continue to use resources with reckless abandon. Everything I need for living is in my van. My goal is to one day live out of a backpack and hope by then that my mode of travel will be equally simplified.

One of my role models for a simple lifestyle is Peace Pilgrim. This beautiful lady, at age 53, walked back and forth across this country for 25 years (covering 25,000 miles) with nothing but the clothes she wore. She was still walking at the age of 81 when she was killed tragically, and ironically, in an auto accident. Her mission was peace. I am taking another mode of travel and my mission concerns our health and the health of the planet, but our hearts beat as one. I only learned of her peace travels after coming to California. Since then I have read her books, watched her documentary and listened to her tapes. I have given away hundreds of her pamphlets, *Steps Toward Inner Peace* and have also visited with John and Ann Rush, Directors of Friends Of Peace Pilgrim, a non-profit organization at 43480 Cedar Ave., Hemet, CA, 92544. Her life has been a great inspiration for me to lead not only a more simple life but also one of peace. If you wish to get more information on Peace Pilgrim's life, contact them for free literature.

Three other great role models for me in living a simple life are Christ, Gandhi, and Martin Luther King. These immortals have made drastic changes in our social and spiritual lives as they lived very simple, nonviolent lives with a message of hope and love. According to Gandhi, this greatness lies deep inside each of us only to be uncovered as we search for the true self, void of the I, Me, and Mine.

I look forward to the day that my pilgrimage offers me the opportunity to live a more simple life in touch with nature. When my body and spirit pass on from this life I pray that my journey shall end as simply as it began. As you continue your search for real meaning in your life please consider a more simple approach to fulfilling your needs. You may be amazed with the response from the Universe and from within your own heart.

Awareness

Awareness can be the most devastating and also the most enlightening word in the English language. It can either destroy us or move us toward the glory of God. In the early 1970s, as I was going through tremendous changes everything I learned put more demands on my already heavily laden shoulders. I was so determined to change my life that awareness seemed to crop up everywhere.

At age 47 I decided to go back to school in the field of social change. One of the courses required me to attend an event in social awareness and I chose a weekend seminar in Monteagle, Tennessee sponsored by the Episcopal Church and centered around a new concept started in California called the Human Potential Movement. I had heard of the cleansing power of this movement and how it could change lives. This movement dealt with every phase of our lives. It involved many issues that faced society of that day. Some of these issues were: deal with feelings, not intellect; if it felt good, do it; female-male relations; open marriage, pot smoking, jealousy, honesty, defensiveness, and a host of other issues that were foreign to many of us in attendance. This movement was not a gentle coaxing to change; it was bang, bang, do it now. Everyone was subject to feedback that could cut to the bone.

Unaware of the issues that I was to encounter, I packed my bag, threw it over my shoulder and set off to Monteagle. In my bag were all the things about my life that I didn't like. I expected to toss all my garbage out into the group, have it massaged, and be rid of it forever. I learned a great lesson that weekend. After 47 years of programming, change does not come easily. Feedback can be cruel and devastating, especially to an innocent, naive, and unsuspecting heart. Now, 27 years later I am still working on some of the garbage that was in my bag on that weekend in 1970. Even though my ego was battered I made a commitment on that day that my life would change. And it has!

This all occurred about the time I had decided I didn't like myself and started on my search for the *real Earle*. I approached this change with a vengeance. There were small group meetings, weekend encounters, and long nights thrashing over all the new data trying to decide what to leave in and what to throw out. I couldn't believe there was so much of my life that needed overhauling.

There were nights I would go home, hide in the bathroom, and cry my heart out. But somehow, the next day I would be right back on the front line. I spent many nights until 3 a.m. sitting on the bed facing my mate discussing such things as trust, defensiveness, jealousy, open marriage, honesty, freedom, and hosts of other feelings that I refused to deal with. I even went to professional counseling for six months searching for help. I went to work some days with little sleep wondering what was awaiting me when I got home. God, those were tough days and tough years. I was determined to change the world and myself along with it.

Without a sizable amount of determination I would

have dropped out and returned to a more comfortable lifestyle. I wondered many times if there was anything worth saving in this devastated body of mine. However, those ego-battering years laid a solid foundation for me as I struggled to break many of the ties with the past. My only surviving friends from those days – 25 years ago – are John and Marilyn Crisler, from Tennessee, who are still very dear to me. (These early years are documented in my autobiography entitled, *A Winner At 60+*.)

For many years I have struggled with this simple little word: awareness. It seemed to be around every corner. I recall striving hard to climb Maslow's Hierarchy Scale toward Self-Actualization as presented in his book, *Motivation and Personality*; or to be a NEZ (non-erroneous zone) person as proposed by Wayne Dyer in his book, *Your Erroneous Zones*; or to build a healthy self-image according to Nathanal Branden's *Psychology of High Self-Esteem*. My early development consisted mostly of self-help material which was primarily concerned with the basic five senses (the ego) and with integrating this into the service that I provided.

As my journey moved more toward acquiring spiritual depth, two things happened; one, that new worlds seemed to open to me leading to a life more in tune with God rather than my own desires. The other was becoming more knowledgeable of all the suffering, pain, and devastation, not only with human life, but also to the planet itself. Thus, as I was becoming more in tune with the spirit, I was also becoming more aware of the physical destruction. I have concluded that it is necessary to confront our own quality of life before we can truly solve problems of our species or the cancer we have caused upon our planet.

Something within me would not let me ignore the

awareness that seemed to be endless. Why couldn't I just be like 'ole' Bessy, the contented cow, that casually strolled across the pasture with her young calf ignoring the world as she grazed. Or why couldn't I be like many humans I know who seem to ignore all spiritual growth and earthly woes, content to live in their own little cocoons? Why did I feel I must respond to all the unfairness and suffering on this earth?

In my early years, I spent my life dealing with my own pain and my own hurt, caused by my very sensitive nature and the immediate environment. My astrological sign is Cancer; the little crab that moves sideways avoiding all confrontation, the one whose tender feelings are always exposed, the one who likes to stay hidden in the corner so as not to become involved, the one that never wants to rock the boat. If Cancer is your sign you may recognize these characteristics. During those changing years I also had to deal with my own personality and finding detours around all those traits within that I didn't like. Throughout the years I have learned to cope with my own personal hurts, but the suffering of others (and the planet) has been more difficult to bear. Ram Dass, one of my spiritual mentors, has helped me understand the necessity and acceptance of such painful experiences, but I still wake up in the middle of the night grieving over the unnecessary pain that afflicts many of the Earth's inhabitants.

Another awareness that has come into focus is the annihilation of the thousands of species that have become extinct during our lifetime. Each of these has played an important part in the continued evolution of life on this planet. We are presently learning the impact of this devastation and only the future will assess the damage to our survival. If we continue to pollute and devastate our environment eventually we will destroy all life on this earth.

Here's an example of how my own awareness has shifted. When I came to California in 1990, my son, knowing the path I was undertaking, gave me a set of Ram Dass cassette tapes. Eagerly I listened but afterwards I returned them to my son as they didn't seem relevant to me at that time. Coming from the deep south, my early religious teachings did not mesh with what I was now hearing. However, as time passed and I became aware of other spiritual teachings, the more God was relevant in my life. Now Ram Dass is one of my spiritual mentors. I am very fortunate for the opportunity to have lived in the Bay Area of California for seven years where there are endless opportunities to choose alternative lifestyles and seek a variety of spiritual options.

This is not to say that I have thrown out all of my early teachings but it has allowed me to expand my understanding of the universe and the nature of God. In my exposure to the Christian faith, Jesus Christ was the centerpiece. I believe that Christ is the greatest example of pure love and compassion that has made the transition from human to spiritual form and I try to live my life in accordance with his teachings. There have been and are many living Saints that give us inspiration and guidance in our search for the most precious jewel of all – that infinitely small spark of pure love that dwells in each of us.

Through meditation, relaxation exercises, and communion with God, many doors open to the beauty that lies beyond. I must sort out each new path as it relates to my own uniqueness and allow myself to flow gently on toward the next door where angels stand to welcome me to a new awareness. I realize that I cannot respond physically to all that becomes available to me but just the deed of becoming aware has an impact on my consciousness which silently guides my future thought processes and actions.

Communications With All Life

On an EarthSave river rafting retreat in California in 1992 an amazing insight was in store for me. At daybreak I sat down to meditate among the rocks along the river path. The river rapids caused a muffled sound in the background and the sun was gradually peeking across the water's edge. As I sat down with my legs crossed I looked down and spotted an egg-shaped speckled rock. As my eyes focused I became totally aware that the rock was alive. No words were spoken, none were necessary.

This incident was an extreme revelation from what I had been aware when my search first began. For most of my life, communication was limited to verbal language and the written word. Also, as we all have experienced, there are non-verbal expressions that many times speak louder than the spoken word. Gradually however, as my awareness broadened my understanding of the connection of all things, I began to understand that it is only natural that this connection would also include communication at all levels.

One of my greatest revelations has been that all matter in this universe is alive and connected, **and** can communicate. Most of us have learned to communicate verbally and non-verbally with one another at the ego level. A few of us now accept that we can communicate at some level with plants and animals; however, to communicate with what we term inanimate objects is totally outside our sphere of acceptance.

To break this barrier we must be well along the path of finding our true selves. We must accept the spiritual concept that all life is connected and that we are only players in God's great plan. And, we must accept that there is a speck of immortality in each of us that is connected at the ultimate point of love.

I am in constant communication with all of my surroundings and carry on a conversation with many "inanimate" objects such as telephone poles, rocks, and the soil. When I am traveling I always take time to talk with my 1990 van. We have an ongoing thing. I am dependent on my van to get me across the country, and my van is dependent on me to give it good mechanical care and love. I know that my van understands and responds accordingly. Sometimes I make up songs and sing to my van. When we arrive at my destination I always give thanks to God and to my van for getting me there safely. Before my van I had a 1981 Subaru registering 230,000 miles without the motor ever being touched. All those years we talked. When I needed a larger vehicle for my travels, I gave it to my friend.

If you are still with me at this point, I would like to take this one step further. When I speak verbally it is because that is my normal ego-state of communication but I must remember that if I want to communicate with the universe, and all therein, I must do it from deep in my heart (at the spiritual level). So, I must go beyond spoken words into the depth of my soul where all things are connected and I must truly care and have compassion to be heard. When we of the human race learn this depth of communication with each other, wars will cease, crime will vanish, and we will live in harmony with the unity of all creation.

There is another aspect of communication that is extremely important if we want to keep our bodies in peak condition. Many years ago I learned what Albert Carter called "The Healthy Cell Concept" consisting of four components; cell exercise, cell environment, cell food, and cell communication. This concept is described in his book, *The Cancer Answer*, where Larry Lymphocyte takes Carter through a wonderful inside trip. I was amazed to learn that not only do cells talk to each other they also respond to our requests. I began collecting other books on the subject and soon learned about our amazing internal universe we have inside and the vital role that communication plays in maintaining it. Today, when I arise I always talk to all my internal organs as though each cell is listening and waiting for my morning greeting. I find that my body responds with much delight and I start my day full of energy.

Our bodies know when we are sincere and they respond accordingly. The more we learn about our body the more it helps us find that elusive spiritual quality embedded deep in the space within our cells.

While our world is in constant verbal communication, it continues to be an uphill struggle for our survival. Only when we are able to communicate from our innermost being will we be able to solve many of our worldly problems. If each of us were to spend an hour a day in touch with our body and our soul, much of our verbal communication could go unspoken.

If you choose such unorthodox types of communication, your friends and family may shy away from you. It takes a lot of ego (or, better yet, no ego at all) to make this a way of life, but it can change your life forever. You might want to start slowly. Try looking into the mirror talking to each of your body organs. Tell them how wonderful they are, how you want to please them, and how you need their help in having a great day. Remember: your cells know whether you are sincere or not. If you really believe then you will have great rewards. After mastering communication with your body, you are ready for the next level.

Go outside and talk to your automobile (looking around to see if anyone is watching), the old oak tree in the backyard, or the caterpillar you almost stepped on. It always helps if you touch (caress) the object of your communication. I find it very helpful to be eyeball – to – eyeball with the other party. If you are afraid of spiders try this. Get as close as you can (or dare) and start talking to the spider. Tell it you want to be its friend, that you understand that it is one of God's creatures, that you are afraid and need its help to overcome your fears, and that in return you will respect its right to life. Each time you see a spider, try this exercise. You may be surprised at what happens to your fear and what happens to your thoughts about all life. This type and level of communication works with all lifeforms and with inanimate objects.

Many years ago, while my wife Pat and I were walking in the woods we came upon what I thought was an ordinary tree, but Pat went up and hugged the tree and sat down and began to weep. Little did I understand. My engineering and logical mind didn't understand at all what was happening between her and the tree. It has taken me many years to recognize the significance of this event and now I also hug trees. It is the recognition that all things are connected and that the tree is alive and far more than just shade or firewood.

I have become more aware of the connection between the mind and the body as well as between the mind and other life forms. As you might know, some people with terminal diseases have healed themselves using mind-body medicine. What you may not be aware of is that with mind/body communication you can also help heal other people's diseases. For example, my son had colon cancer six years ago. The doctors had taken out the upper section of his colon. What followed was the trauma of waiting for the doctor's prognosis. About this time I was listening to a set of tapes by Dr. Robert Stone on mind/body communication and felt very strongly that I could help my son's recovery and healing. Using some of Dr. Stone's approach, I would spend hours sending messages from my own mind and body to my son's, convinced that I could help him rid himself of this disease forever. I surely don't take all the credit but I'm convinced that my efforts and prayers helped him recover. Now six years later my son is cancer free. I do believe that this communication must come from deep within the heart, at the cellular level, the space within the cells where the spirit abides.

There are many, many approaches to communication at the cellular level. You may have heard of the dowsing technique which has been used for generations in locating water. This art has now been expanded to communicate within the cellular levels in the body for health, diagnosis, and healing, and is used by some doctors to help locate and assist in healing. Most of these doctors use a variety of terms in lieu of dowsing as this technique is not accepted in the medical establishment. Yet for believers and practitioners, such as myself, it has performed miracles.

If you go to your local bookstore or attend alternative healing expositions you will find many methods for healing the mind, the body, and the spirit. All of these are a matter of communication at some deeper level. There is no question in my mind that the body is the best healer of itself; but this concept requires a considerable shift from our normal medical approach to healing. There is an additional benefit in letting our bodies do the talking *and listening* – we don't have to learn different languages. At the soul level there is no racial, color, or language barrier and all is perfectly understood.

A beautiful true love story is told in Brian Weiss's, *Only Love is Real*. Weiss used hypnosis to unveil the past of two of his patients who in fact were related in past lives and who had re-discovered each other in their present life. I was astounded. I am open to all the mysteries of life and beyond, and accept all without question, but this is far beyond my fundamental understanding. It does open up new avenues to explore as my search for the *real Earle* continues.

I know this type of communication is new to most people. Just let it soak in slowly, and if you are a person-to-person verbal communicator at this point that's okay. It may grab you one day as it did me. Many times now I don't speak verbally. If I'm at a deeper level of communication, my soul relays the message and can do a much better job of it than I can verbally. So, if you're up to it, give it a try.

Two Magnificent Universes

During my 35 year career as an engineer in NASA's Space Program, I had ample time to view and study the universe. Of course, I am speaking of the magnificent universe in which our planet Earth is but one speck in one galaxy in this enormous field we call space. It is not my intention to use this book to speak of the magnitude or of the mechanics of this enormous gift of God. These cosmic mechanics have been documented by many experts on the theories and evolution of our galaxies, using the mathematical and physical laws that keep all elements in orbit, including our own solar system.

One of the big payoffs of my involvement in the Space Program was the opportunity, as part of the moon exploration, to view this beautiful blue planet as it was beamed back to us. It was an awesome sight. Today, when this scene has been viewed by countless millions it is hard to convey the spell that many of us experienced at that time. I recall my first thoughts were that I could see no boundaries, no wars, and no inhabitants. It looked so serene hanging there in space. The image had a most profound spiritual impact on me, as it did on many others in the Space Program. I could not erase this view from my mind.

Why, I kept asking myself, can't we hold the astounding impression of this scene in our minds and our hearts as we live our daily lives?

I began to question many views that I had, relating not only to the real world, but to the true meaning of life on earth. What was the relationship between this real world and the true essence of life? In my engineering world there are formulas and facts that dictate our understanding of the mechanics of our universe. But what of that part that is unseen and does not lend itself to the same laws that govern what we see, this nebulous thing we call our spirit?

Since I had some concept of the fabulous universe that surrounds us, I wanted to know more about the universe within, the physics and the chemistry that lets us function as human beings. Whatever I had learned in school was mostly lost because I wasn't too concerned about how my body functioned on the inside but rather how it operated as a total entity. I had taken it all for granted.

With help of the electron microscope and TV documentaries (such as Discovery) slowly I became aware of each of the organs and their functions and was amazed at how complex our bodies really are. I became engrossed in studying each organ of the body and its relationship to all other organs and to the total functioning of the body. As I focused deeper and deeper into our structure it finally became apparent that there was also a magnificent universe within. Of course, physicists, doctors, and other learned people have been aware of this for ages but for me it was a tremendous 'Aha'. As I compared the inner universe with the outer universe I realized that the two were linked. Cells, atoms, and molecules form solar systems within, consistent with the magnitude and distances observed in our own solar system and the galaxies.

I was totally overwhelmed with what I was learning. I could envision over five billion individual universes trodding around on our planet with the complexities that can be observed only with our electron microscopes. Each of us has a built-in computer more complex than our best known computers. The facts alone are enormous: billions of galaxies, each with billions of stars with untold solar systems that could support life of some sort; the 100 trillion cells (solar systems) that make up each of our bodies, each one already schooled in its particular function, carrying out the daily duties as assigned. And how immense is all that space between molecules? Experts today tell us that our bodies are made up of 99.99+ percent space. That means physically that if this space were filled with mass, each of us could weigh hundreds of thousands of pounds. Another way of putting it might be that if you had a truck load of marbles and you took out a few and held them in your hand, that few would represent your total mass, the rest of the marbles represent space!

The space within all these cells is not empty but rather contains all the information available to us. We know of magnetic fields, electron fields, microwaves, radio waves, light rays, and many other media. We have learned to bring these to life through our senses such as sight and hearing. Previously I had only considered these universes from a mechanical view. Another great 'Aha' had come into my awareness, that within these spaces the Spirit of God also dwells. This presence comes alive within our heart or soul through awareness. If we attune ourselves to the right frequency and listen for this "still small voice" the message can be heard. Most of us go through life unaware of the spiritual messages that are always present because we are not tuned to the right frequency. It is not my intention to go further into this because it is a debatable subject that fills our libraries. Enough to say here is that the spirit of God dwells within each of us and our souls are filled with this infinite love.

With our technology we can actually tour the body at the cellular level and see what is happening inside our organs. Doctors can perform operations with lasers and medical probes that are astounding. The more I became aware of my body, the more I became determined to find the source of this miraculous temple we call our body. In my mind, I cannot fathom anyone who is even moderately aware of our own inner universe, who does not believe in, and search for, the source of all creation.

If we could but fathom the hundreds of millions of years through evolution that has bestowed upon us this great honor to be alive with this miraculous universe within, we would no longer take this gift for granted. I began my trip inward with the desire to understand the mechanics of our bodies, how each organ performed its function to keep us alive and healthy. I was totally awed as each organ perfectly performed its function. Can you imagine the hundreds of operations that go on just to get out of bed in the morning, to get ready for work, to drive a car, or play any sport, or heal ourselves? In a healthy body these functions occur in perfect harmony with every other cell and organ within the body. It will astound you as it did me, to learn about this fabulous immune system that – like the most perfect army ever developed – protects us from all the adversities of our environment. We could not live one day without the protection of this vast army.

The more I learned about this magnificent universe within the more I appreciated it and the more I wanted to take care of it. From Albert E. Carter's *The Cancer Answer*, I learned the four essentials of having healthy cells and therefore a healthy body – exercise, communication, environment, and food. Through this process my body responded and I began to feel more alive.

At this time I was introduced (by Carter) to the small round trampoline called a rebounder. I began to rebound at least an hour each day. I would jog, dance, ski, and perform a variety of exercises that energized every cell in my body. Of all the exercise equipment on the market I would choose the rebounder as the single-most effective. Today, when possible, I carry a fold-up model in my van.

The more I grew aware of the physical properties of my body the more I began to wonder what was behind this most intricate and most magnificent creation. My mind was now ready to venture into the unknown, the spirit world, to help me search deeper into the meaning of all life, searching for the *real Earle*.

It is well within our technical expertise today to view an article the size of a dime from hundreds of miles in space. Nothing on earth seems to be able to escape our scrutiny. We also have the technology, through our electron microscopes, to view our inner universe in operation and even take a trip to the remote recesses of our body.

I often envision myself very high above a large city with a giant telescope and microscope at my side. At this great height the city appears serene with no activity and only an occasional cloud shading parts of the city. It is hardly distinguishable from its surroundings and shows no hint of discomfort. If I were from another world I might pass it by as it blended into the environment, not worth another look. But as you and I know, there is a real hustle and bustle going on at the street level.

To get past the street level of living I now pick up my electron microscope to shift from outer-space to inner-space. As I travel from organ to organ and watch them perform miracles to keep our bodies functioning, I realize that our bodies are in the midst of two great universes. The outer one contains billions of galaxies and each galaxy contains billions of stars. The inner universe contains billions of galaxies with billions of stars that we call cells. In fact, each of our bodies contains between 60 and 75 trillion cells. This number is beyond our comprehension. We could give each living human 15,000 of our cells and still have a sizable amount left over. Yet each cell knows exactly where it is to be placed and what function to carry out. And to think that this all started from one cell after the miraculous combining of a sperm and an egg.

The more I learn about my own physical body the more I appreciate it and the more I am awed that God would allow us to host this magnificent delicate universe. As I write this the news headlines proclaim we now have the ability to clone sheep, and a chemist claims he has the knowledge to clone a human being. No doubt, it will happen in our lifetime. We have now taken evolution completely out of the picture, although some will say this is just evolution at an accelerated pace.

My search continues to unfold the mysteries of myself, the universe, and thus, God. With each 'Aha' I am more inspired to open my universe within to become one with the universe without. What a marvelous journey!

Meditation

I have spent endless hours sitting in the redwoods or on the beach at sunrise in total silence opening my heart and listening for that "still small voice." At times the response comes in more awareness of nature, and at other times, more insight into my own connection with all things. At other times I seem to connect deeper into the spiritual realm, the essence of the universe. Occasionally, a truly great 'Aha' comes through that opens a new door in my search for the *real Earle*.

There are times, mostly when I'm in the woods and always alone, that I feel like I have had a "near death" experience without the preceding physical trauma that most people experience – at least those that have returned to tell us about it. I don't see it as a light at the end of the tunnel but I truly have transcended the self. There is a communion that comes at no other time. It does not come at those times when I am petitioning God, but rather those times when there is a near void of consciousness, even thought. For me these become rare as my mind constantly wants to interfere. Much of this book is being written after such experiences.

It frustrates me that when I translate these experiences into words it is never the same as the experiences themselves. I wish I could relate the exact meaning of such encounters – I would have a best seller and I would truly touch your heart. Most of my life experiences in being a "social robot" have greatly inhibited my communication skills and sometimes God has to knock extra hard just to get my attention.

As I look back on my deep involvement with the organized church, I realize that much of it was an ego trip for me where others set the agenda. I was so involved with saving others I failed to concentrate on myself. During my career with the Space Program I learned that one of our biggest problems in reaching the heavens was in overcoming Earth's gravity. I now understand that my biggest obstacle in reaching the heavens is overcoming the gravity generated by trying to live up to other people's expectations. I have found that through meditation, gradually I am more able to break loose from this gravity and to be transcended directly into space (within and without). I am learning also that discipline and time are required to remove me from the noisy world outside and the continuous thought process inside.

Earlier in my life my contact with God was through prayer. Primarily, prayer was used at meals, at bedtime, and in religious activities. Other times it might have been appropriately related in response to fear, ecstasy, and death. Prayer worked best when I folded my hands (prayer hands), looked toward heaven or kneeled, and bowed my head. Today, looking back, I'm not sure of God's reaction to my prayers but I think mostly I was sincere in my requests or thanksgiving. At the time I was praying to a God outside my body. I think inwardly my heart was touched. I believe God was reaching me even though I wasn't aware of it.

For me, as a Christian, the way to eternal life was praying to God through Jesus Christ. I accepted this without question in my early life but as I grew older I began to question many of the church's teachings. Eventually, this resulted in distrust and ended in my separation from the organized church. In my opinion it wasn't God's church, it had become man's church. For 25 years I have hoped for a reconciliation with the organized church but, at this time, the odds seem slim.

I do believe that God speaks to us – many times loudly and clearly – in a medium not considered to be meditation. In tragedies, emergencies, and illnesses a door seems to open offering an opportunity to come inside. These incidents are generally caused by fear and not a genuine effort on our part. At other times we seem to transcend our physical bodies effortlessly. As an example, I have been an avid runner most of my life and there have been times when I have run a mile or two without any recollection of going anywhere or feeling physical exhaustion. I seemed to have transcended into another world, and it was a wonderful experience. The minute I became grounded again I could feel the strain and pain of my body. I began to wonder how I might be in this transcended state more often.

Before I go further I must give my understanding of meditation and how this correlates to both prayer and communion with God. For me, my prayers were generally a petition or thanksgiving with the one we call God, up there somewhere in Heaven sitting on **HIS** throne. Since I have become more "sophisticated" I now use the term meditation instead of prayer, because I associate the word prayer with organized religion. We used to have prayer meetings on Wednesday at church; now I meditate. I now realize that prayer and meditation are one and the same, and both are a means of communion with God. Sometimes I feel that meditation is more of a condition, an aura, which engulfs my whole being and, as such, I am in meditation all of the time. I know people who continually seem to be engulfed in God and you can feel that presence.

I still remember the time in one of our men's Bible study classes that someone asked the question, "where is God?" One of my friends reached over and lifted the lid on the sugar bowl and asked, "God are you there"? Of course, he was being facetious but that incident struck a chord within me. Surely, if God was in the sugar bowl then God was everywhere, even within me. It now became a more personal issue and communion was a mutual participation between God and myself. At that point our relationship was on a 50-50 basis where I learned God's will for me, and strived to carry it out. In more recent years I have learned that through meditation only God does the speaking. By this I mean that, by listening, I become more in tune with the true spiritual nature of the Universe and also how to be more God-like in my service in the real world. As my spirit is transformed, so is my service.

I believe that the spirit world opens to us in many different ways; however, as an ongoing practice of becoming more effective in our ego-oriented society, disciplined meditation is by far the best approach. I have scarcely touched the knowledge of the Saints and the great Masters in learning the discipline of meditation. In 1995, I attended a meditation retreat at the Blue Mountain Retreat Center in Tomales, California to learn more of the techniques that could aid in my quest. This center was established by Eknath Easwaran in 1959 when he came to this country from India on a Fulbright scholarship. He is a scholar of Eastern philosophy, religion, and is very prominent in the Indian teachings of the Bhagavad Gita. It was an honor to be in his presence.

In my youth God was someone to be feared. Evangelists offered us hell-fire, brimstone, and damnation if we did not obey God. HE was not a God of love but one to fear. Through Christ we found solace in the message of love, kindness, and forgiveness; however, if we wished to reach salvation, that was to come through the crucifixion, death, and resurrection of Jesus Christ (the Trinity). After spending the past eight years in California, many, many new spiritual horizons have opened for me. I am enjoying a spiritual freedom in my search for the *real Earle* that I never dreamed existed. So as not to discourage those of you who don't live in the San Francisco Bay Area, please know that the search for your spiritual freedom is a personal and inward search and may be found anywhere you are on this planet. Because of the many spiritual teachers, masters, gurus and spiritual centers in this area, you might wish to consider a visit to one in the future, primarily to be in the presence of others on the same path and to learn from those who have been on the path for many years.

I must emphasize the importance of sincere time spent in connecting with the one true spirit, the God of Love. Whether we call it meditation, quiet time, relaxation, prayer, or any other name, we won't find the true self unless we find a way to transcend this ego state which dominates our daily lives. I believe that the paths leading to the spiritual universe are varied and endless. I find that my day of service is more filled with compassion, love, and understanding if I have at least an hour a day in deep communion with God. As I travel across the country I have an excellent opportunity to absorb my natural surroundings and to keep in close communion with God. I also have hundreds of cassette tapes and many books that expand my knowledge and bring awareness right into my soul.

This past Thanksgiving was a unique experience for me. The previous day I attended a turkey-free dinner presented by the Local EarthSave Group in Miami, Florida. These meat-free events are a real treat that are happening more and more across the country. You might consider a turkey-free dinner in the future. On Thanksgiving day I chose to fast and spend the day in seclusion and in meditation, giving thanks for all the blessings I continually receive. My day started at dawn on the shores of Miami Beach. What a beautiful way to begin the day. The beach was almost deserted except for a few early morning beachcombers. Settling down facing the east where the sun would soon be peeking through the fluffy clouds, I chose to start my day in silent meditation. I could feel God's presence becoming more intense as the world slowly faded into the background.

The sun rose higher in the sky and warmed my chilled body and my silent meditation turned to giving thanks for my many blessings. Afterwards, I chose to focus on individuals who have influenced my life. One by one, I brought each of these people into my consciousness, and while viewing them face-to-face, I offered special thanks for their lives and, especially, for the impact of their lives on me. After hundreds of face-to-face contacts I was totally transcended onto another plane, one in which only angels abound. A beautiful aura surrounded my life. The experience was so captivating that, I confess I was annoyed when the rising sun and noisy beachcombers brought me back to reality.

As the day continued, I chose places which were more secluded to continue my meditative state. Only in moments of reality was I aware that I was in a fasting mode which prompted me to return to the quietness of the spiritual state. By the time the day was complete I had spent time in a variety of meditative states including quiet time listening for that "still small voice", time in giving thanks, time in open communication with God, time in petition for those in desperate need in our world, and concluded with the verbal repetition of the Prayer of St. Francis for 30 minutes.

What a beautiful and awe-inspiring day! At such times my thoughts are drawn toward the monastic life, one in which I could spend each day in quiet contemplation, in constant search where peak experiences are routine. But my dharma keeps calling me back to a life of service among the ills (and the blessings) of our society. However, one day I shall treat myself with a six-month stay in an ashram where every day shall be Thanksgiving.

As a side note to meditation, I will describe my association with my mantra. This is generally one word or a short phrase repeated over and over when frustrated, a bit angry, alienated from the spirit, or just as an offering of love. This is used to re-attach you to the spirit when you are doing your normal ego stuff. I have chosen the word Ram, which means God. This was constantly on the tongue of Gandhi – the last words he uttered when he was assassinated. As Gandhi is one of my great spiritual mentors, I have chosen also to use that mantra.

Use of the mantra has been a great experience for me in which I have found many rewards. I use this at a variety of times. As an example I will repeat "Ram" over and over when I ride my bike leisurely in the mornings. I have used a variety of tunes, some make sense, some don't and, at times, I find myself getting very exuberant (and loud) as I'm almost shouting "Ram, Ram, Ram, Ram." I am aware that sometimes people stare at me as though I was some kook from California (which I am) but, being that I was raised in the deep south, I immediately become self-conscious and crawl into my shell. About a block down the way I start again, a little more wary. At least, I was saying "Ram, Ram, Ram" instead of "God, God, God" and most people don't recognize that term so they don't think me so weird. When I am among the California redwoods I feel more comfortable doing my mantras, as that is an accepted part of the behavior there.

This can be a very spiritual experience, so I invite you to choose a mantra for yourself and see how you respond. One of the best ways to start is when you feel your level of anxiety increasing, just step off to the side and repeat your mantra over and over for a while. It will have a calming effect and the adverse situation will be perceived differently.

As you are aware by now, meditation (prayer) has become an important episode in my search for the *real Earle*. As I peel away more and more layers of the physical and intellectual bondage of my ego, there lies the naked spirit of God, inviting me to experience even more of the beauty of the essence of love.

At the Blue Mountain Retreat I learned a new approach to meditation. Rather than conversing with God or being in total silence, I was asked to pick a certain expression that was meaningful to me and had great spiritual significance, one that had weathered the ages and was universal in its message. I chose the Prayer of St. Francis. I was asked to repeat this prayer over and over for 30 minutes each morning as my meditation and, if possible, again at night. At first I was a little skeptical as it didn't seem to allow me to hear the "still small voice" that I was always tuned in for. Further, it was suggested that I speak very slowly and deliberately, accenting key words and pausing between phrases to allow it to sink deep into my soul.

I conclude this chapter on meditation with the Prayer of St. Francis and the serenity it has offered my life. I trust that you may also establish your own approach to communion with God and make it a priority in your life.

Prayer of St. Francis

God, let me be an instrument of Thy Peace
Where there is hatred, let me sow love
Where there is injury, pardon
Where there is doubt, faith
Where there is despair, hope
Where there is darkness, light
Where there is sadness, joy.

O Divine Spirit,
Grant that I may not so much seek
To be consoled as to console,
To be understood as to understand,
To be loved as to love;
For it is in giving that we receive;
It is in pardoning that we are pardoned;
It is in dying of self
that we are born to eternal life.

After a year of using this approach, I am astonished at the results. This prayer has become a part of my being, and my response to the world is more acute. My days are more in tune with the spirit and, therefore, my service. At times during the day, I find myself repeating one or more of the lines as time permits.

You who are not of the Christian faith may also find that this prayer goes beyond all religious boundaries and penetrates deep into the universal spirit. Again, you may choose any expression that more closely fits your own experiences. I still plan to use other types of meditation as my moods or needs warrant. As you search deeper into your spiritual connection I pray you will consider some form of daily quiet time where you might be alone with your God and see what your day holds in store for you.

Life on the Road

After spending five years learning all that I could about EarthSave, working at the organization's headquarters (then in Santa Cruz) as a full-time volunteer, I have spent the past three years traveling this country spreading the EarthSave message and raising the consciousness of how our food choices and how many of our diseases and environmental problems are determined by our eating habits. Traveling across the country as the Earth-Save Ambassador also gives me an opportunity to find new avenues in my search for the *real Earle*. Meeting new people, being more in touch with nature, and more time to be alone in a meditative state, has opened new doors for me.

How fortunate I was to have had five years in Santa Cruz where my life changed dramatically. I often tell people that you haven't experienced life until you spend five years in Santa Cruz. Even though my lifestyle fit in nicely when I arrived in California I had no concept of what lay in store for me. Santa Cruz is a place where you can create your own lifestyle and the University of California at Santa Cruz (UCSC) students provide a youthful voice in political and environmental change. Where could you find a more serene place to be a part of nature and voice for future generations?

Traveling has added a new experience to my search. As

I travel it has been a great joy to observe what millions of years has provided us as a livable planet for us humans to share and enjoy. To our present knowledge we are the only life to be so privileged. The abundance of wild life that surrounds us was put here long before we emerged as a human species. The great variety of trees, wild flowers, and grasses that cover our planet where millions of species call home. The environment with its proper balance of weather, temperature, water, and air that makes this a living planet; everything exquisitely tuned to support all life on the earth.

This is my view of creation as I travel across the wide countryside, searching for the pristine lands still not invaded by our industrialized society. These places still exist if we are willing to wander far from our cities, interstates, and massive construction sites that cover our land. I only pray that we can somehow come to a balance between machines and the environment and stop the flow of concrete and the destruction of our natural habitat.

I carry my bike with me on most of my trips. Not only is it more ecological but the bike can carry me where my car can't. Also it provides me with exercise that I don't get while I'm in my van. Sometimes I park both my van and my bike and walk which gets me even closer to our natural state. Walking allows me to stop along the way and get down and eyeball the wild flowers and the small insects that are always near by. I just sit and thank God for the many blessings that exist, some of them right below our noses but we don't stop long enough to appreciate.

I realized many years ago that my search would lead me across all boundaries and even into the Universe itself. I have a large name tag which reads, 'Earle Harris, World Citizen', that I wear wherever I travel. In being a slow moving person from the deep south, where change happens slowly, I am not one to denounce my US citizenship, but in my head and in my heart I believe in one world where there are no boundaries, and that all people and all life is just as important in God's view as my next door neighbor or even my family. It grieves me to see so much of our society and our politics committed to protecting our own boundaries and gluttonous living at the huge cost to the peoples of the world, and to the planet itself. The deeper I search for my true being the more this is relevant for me.

Part of my calling of the road is to cross as many boundaries as possible with a message to all people, and to experience as much of the sacred beauty of our land as possible. This past trip across the country, as I traveled on I-24 through western Kentucky, I became acutely aware that something was missing. There were no billboards! What a joy. It was a beautiful drive and I felt very warm inside. I enjoyed the 100-mile drive thinking how thoughtful that someone had seen to it that this blight would not be a part of this very scenic drive.

A drastic change in scenery takes place as you head toward Florida. All the way down I-75 there is a continuous row of billboards advertising the great playground of Florida. If you are a tourist these become very important to both you and the economy of Florida. I cannot fault this condition too much because, in my previous traveling days as a tourist, I would scan these billboards for sight-seeing opportunities and cheap hotel accommodations. Anyway, today they stand out as a blight on our landscape and tell much about what is important in our society today. But there are many wonderful natural things available for those who venture there.

As I cross the Colorado Rockies I notice the snow-covered mountains with an occasional tree above the tree line and above all the other trees, and I wonder how that lone tree was able to survive without the protection of all the others. Then the thought occurred to me that it is like an occasional person who stands out beyond the crowd ready to brave the elements so that we may all may benefit. I envision myself being one of those trees, then I smile. Also, I would see people along the highway picking up trash. If traffic permitted I would slow down, wave and say thank you. Some of them would only stare back in disbelief.

A most memorable sight stands out during my recent Miami visit. As I crossed over the McArthur causeway onto Miami Beach, I was stunned to see five cruise ships moored along the Miami Port all in a row, a truly magnificent sight. Late that evening, just before dusk as I took a bike ride on South Beach, to my surprise, the Carnival Celebrity cruise ship was passing out the inlet. It was as though I could almost reach out and touch it. I stood in total amazement as it truly looked like a carnival with lights glistening and the decks filled with waving crowds as it sailed off into the Atlantic (and I forgot my camera). For a moment I forgot my mission in Florida and stood in silent awe of what our technology offers us for a few relaxing days basking in the sun and living a life of leisure. And I thought to myself, would I ever allow such luxury for me? We shall see.

I have been instrumental in starting six EarthSave Local Groups in Florida. This is my main mission, to be a pilgrim in presenting our message and organizing local groups empowered to make positive changes in their communities. I find that there are many individuals across our land ready to make a difference, just waiting for someone to organize and lead.

I try to avoid the interstate highways when time permits and travel the more scenic paths. Highway 89A from Flagstaff to Sedona is one of the most impressive sights I've seen. Plan to go 25 miles per hour and see the beautiful rock mountains as the western sun makes a golden view. Or travel highway 60 from Phoenix through Salt Flat Canyon into New Mexico. Nature provides so many beautiful pristine places but wherever it is profitable for humankind then it is slowly eaten away. We are spreading cancerous pockets all across our land. When I stop to relax in some of these natural wonders I am awed by these great gifts but am saddened by the way we treat our pristine lands. I cannot help asking the age old question, why? Will our greed be the end of our species?

Even though it is a great opportunity to see our land, my life on the road is more than a scenic tour. This is how I am able to fulfill my purpose in life, to be a servant wherever there is a need. As I travel full time I have broken my need to be a citizen of a particular state. Of course, for voting, taxes, and automobile tags I must legally be attached to somewhere, but in my mind I am attached to nowhere. Before I die, I expect to see country after country relax its borders as Europe has done in recent years. And, who knows, this could spread to continents. In this country we must first accomplish this at our northern and southern borders. I look forward to the day when we accept all people as our brothers and sisters. Unfortunately, before that happens we may be forced to live together because of economics and over- population rather than love.

This gives you an idea of some of the things that fill my time as I travel, sometimes as much as twelve hours at a stretch. In all my life I have never been bored with traveling. I have hundreds of tapes that keep me motivated and inspired, and I sometimes go for an hour in dead silence, just absorbing nature. Then, at other times I am concentrating on my heart, giving thanks for the many blessings that shower down upon me. Please remember that I never allow myself to drift away from my responsibilities of the road and safety, and where traffic requires it I concentrate on my driving. If I feel tired I always stop at rest stops to stretch and sometimes even take a short nap.

One phase of my career was during the oil embargo of the early 1970s. I traveled to many of the National Parks to install solar systems in the visitor centers to determine the feasibility of the use of solar for energy in place of oil. This gave me the opportunity to see firsthand some of our pristine lands that were set aside to protect our natural resources. It was an opportunity for me to experience nature in its natural state blessed with history of hundreds and thousands of years. Today it is a different sight as so many of our sanctuaries are being exploited and trashed.

Traveling across Wyoming you can go for miles and see nothing but yourself and then come to a sign stating "population 14". And if you get off the main highways you can see six-foot wheel ruts worn by the earlier settlers traveling west and sheltered areas where they camped. As far as you can see there are no telephone poles or power lines stretched across the terrain. I ponder the life of the early Americans and the hardships that they endured as they established the western frontier. I think of the great buffalo herds that roamed the land and of the indians who were being pushed further into isolated reservations. I think to myself, what a price has been paid so I might enjoy this fabulous land in which we live.

As I travel the west coast from northern California to Washington state and see the clear-cutting of our forests my heart cries out in shame. If you have ever traveled through the redwood forests and seen these magnificent giants – some a thousand years old, 20 feet in diameter, and 300 feet high – you wonder why we would ever allow even one to be cut. A wonderful experience awaits you if you ever have the opportunity to travel the Avenue of the Giants in northern California.

The more I travel the more connected I become to this wonderful land and the more I want to protect it from the claws of economic development and industrialization. We should be thankful that in this country we have a strong environmental movement which fights to preserve our land and all life that dwells upon it. Much of our planet (especially the Third World) is being threatened by survival, greed, and industrialization and protecting the environment is not high on the list.

I was in the Naval Air Corps during WW II and got to see the islands that dot the Pacific Ocean and the devastation that was caused. The environment didn't seem to be important at that time as our interests were in survival. I am happy today that I might travel in peace but now I recognize the cancer that we are creating for our planet. At times I pull off into a viewing area and sit for thirty minutes looking across our great land and, with tears in my eyes, wonder what more I can do to help preserve this earth from needless gouging because of our greed.

The road has been good for me and maybe some day

Free Spirit

The Search for the Real Earle

On the road

Speaking in Vancouver Canada

PHOTOS BY MILTON NOEY

Red letter day

The Search for the Real Earle

"Earle's Grove

With author John Robbins

Miami Zoo

Ram Dass, Western Guru and Mentor

The Search for the Real Earle

*Me and my son Keith,
California Style*

Tennessee Family at Christmas time

*Me and Eleanor,
my spiritual Mentor*

John Robbins and I struggle for Kayak, I lost

The Search for the Real Earle

Grand Daughter Jinny

Yours truly, and the Robbins family, Deo, Ocean, John and Michelle

our paths will cross and we will swap stories of this great land of ours. I pray that one day we may establish peace across our planet where all may enjoy and benefit from the gifts of our land.

Life on the road is not all a bed of roses. While on my last trip across the country I began to have joint problems which were quite painful. I managed, with some difficulty, to get back to Santa Cruz where I knew I could get many types of alternative help, which I prefer. I am definitely against drugs as a cure and I am continuing my own alternative approaches to find a more suitable cure. For most of my adult life I have rarely had so much as a cold, even though I smoked for 25 years before the health effects were known. For a person who has always been in excellent health, these joint problems are a very embarrassing thing to happen to me. I am humbled and can appreciate what has become a serious health problem for an estimated 40 million Americans.

As I believe very strongly that the body is its own best healer, it is a great opportunity for me to improve my own defenses and allow my body to heal itself. As I also believe in meditation, prayer and miracles, I will give this top priority in my approach to the healing process. Philosophically I believe that when I have learned the lesson meant for me God will send the angels to cleanse my body. I am learning to slow down, be more patient, and more compassionate for the millions of people who suffer from joint problems. I am not bitter and accept this as a positive step to improve my health for the future. I have improved immensely in the past few months and by the time you read this I shall be back on the road again continuing my service to our planet.

Nature As My Teacher

I felt very close to nature as a youngster and remember sitting under an old hackberry tree in the back yard watching the squirrels and the birds playing in the treetops with an occasional butterfly or cricket nearby. I used to daydream about being a bird or animal because they were free and had no enemies (or so I thought at the time). The stories I heard in school were those that showed animals as loving pets, with an occasional "ole bad wolf" thrown in. Also, I can remember the open fields down by the railroad tracks where I would go and sit observing nature, seeing it as my hiding place. I grew up very protective of animals and when others would be unkind I would follow behind trying to correct the situation. When others would put baby kittens in mailboxes and close the lids, I would come by later and release them. I was not a confrontational lad so chose to undo rather than confront.

A horror that still haunts me was an incident when visiting my wife's home in Arkansas. We stopped at a country store and, as we were leaving, several young fellows set fire to a possum that was sulking in front of the store. I was horrified wondering how they could do such a thing. Instead of confronting the boys I got in my car and drove on. After 50 years I still can't shake that incident.

How often do we observe such horror and drive away justifying it as none of our business?

As the years rolled on I became an occasional hunter, forgetting my earlier years and justifying my killing as putting food on the table. By then World War II had ended and killing – even people – had been somehow justified, so it seemed only minor to kill animals for food. My hunting days ended in 1954 when I sat on a tree stump in the woods at daybreak. Quietly life began to stir and I sat with my trusty old double-barreled shotgun ready to fire. In short order a number of squirrels were coming out of their dens and ready to hunt nuts for their winter storage. Without moving I shot five squirrels. As they lay all around me, my earlier years of protecting animals brushed through my mind. I sat for a few moments then went to gather my game. As I looked at each squirrel I was devastated. Each one had a disease caused by not having sufficient cold weather, and were not edible. My youth finally caught up with me and I sat there stunned. I began to cry and ask myself, "What have you done?" That was over 40 years ago and I haven't hunted since. Today as I'm recalling this grim experience tears are rolling down my cheeks.

Today I see nature as my companion and friend. From my house in Santa Cruz, I can be at the beach in five minutes to watch the sunrise and I can be in the redwoods in ten minutes. The sun is my energy and the redwoods my inspiration. Just this morning I sat in a circle of redwoods looking up at the perfectly straight trees that grow hundreds of feet into the sky. Some of these trees have been around for hundreds of years. Each circle has the remains of a mother tree in the center. Mostly redwoods sprout from the roots of the mother tree and grow in a circle as though to protect the mother tree in her old age. For me, this is a perfect place to commune with the spirits. I have received much of my inspiration by sitting and listening for that "still small voice". Rarely do I come out of the woods without some new insight. Sometimes my thoughts turn sad as I recall what we humans are doing to our environment and to all the species that depend on natural habitat for their survival. For our own survival, both as individuals and as a society, we would do well to spend more time in nature away from the technology and industrialization that is slowly consuming and polluting our planet.

If you ever spend much time in nature, you cannot escape the recognition that this is where most species on earth live. Unfortunately, they cannot live where we have devastated their habitat, and so, thousands of species become extinct each year. More and more people are beginning to understand that each and every species is important in the natural progression of all life. Each life is dependent upon other lives and when this chain is broken it has repercussions on other species. Destruction of our forests is one of the blackest marks against humanity.

My time in nature has provided much of the inspiration for this book. For me it is a time of escaping the ego and transcending to another plateau, one of complete love beyond any known expression on this planet. When I travel it is always a pleasure to find quiet time to connect with nature and mingle with the angels – that is where my heart yearns to be, not just for me but for all life on this earth.

From All – I Have Learned

From every person in my life I have learned. From some I have learned how to, from others how not to! But from every person there is a lesson to be gained. Only in recent years have I recognized that every incident in my life has brought me to be exactly who I am today. Many years ago, when I didn't like who I was becoming, it seemed that I discarded many of the inputs of others as being hurtful, negative, and wrong. Now I recognize the value of all my experiences. All have contributed to creating the person I live with each moment, the person I like, and even love.

As a young man I was very active in the community and the church and received a lot of positive feedback. I was a leader in many activities because I was unable to say no. I was determined to overcome my fear of failure and be more than a spectator. In those days most of my praise came from my accomplishments, not from the person I was inside, as that was my thrust at that time.

I am no longer critical of any event or person in my life. If anything had been different, I would not be the person that I am today. I have a saying posted in my van which reads, "In My Life There Are No Problems – Only Opportunities". That's a tough one to live up to but if I stop a moment and think, I usually can approach any situation with a positive attitude.

I have often thought that much of my life was not aligned with the goals that I had set for myself. I know now the paths that I have taken have been right for me and allowed me to grow at a productive pace. If I take the time to see the conditions and environment in which I spent my youth, I can only marvel at the person I am today. Many times I look in the mirror and smile.

My dad was a strict, intolerant, authoritarian who caused me to fear him and we never had a close relationship. He was rather typical of the male society of the early 1900s. He grew up under tough conditions after the turn of the century on a farm in Tennessee, was a soldier during World War I, and adjusted to the strict military values of the day. I don't remember a day when he was not in control, especially where his immediate family was concerned. I had every right to hate my father, but I don't recall ever having hateful feelings for him. In many ways, in my younger life, I shared many of his traits (but with more tolerance). I often remember with regret the horrors that I imposed on my own children in their young and tender years. Somehow they survived such harsh treatment and have made respectful positions in life, and for me three wonderful granddaughters.

Though not aware of it at the time, I learned responsibility, loyalty, and determination from my dad which has paid off big time in achieving my goals. From my mom I learned patience and the gift of facilitating which she constantly did between my dad and me. Both of my parents died at the young age of 53 so I don't know what wisdom I have missed as a result of their early deaths.

I have learned much from books and tapes that have guided me along my spiritual path. In recent years the quality of the people with whom I have associated have given me the love and courage to continue my search and to be proud of who I am. One of the greatest needs that I have is the positive feedback I receive from so many people. Many times I have been embarrassed by the accolades that have come my way. I feel strongly that I am not worthy of praise but it nurtures my soul. My elegant friend Eleanor, who has just turned 90, often introduces me to her friends as an angel. I know in my heart that I am no angel but it does inspire me to be all that I can be.

I am blessed with a daughter, Kathy, and a son Keith, who love, respect, and honor me in spite of my crazy California ways. I know they both care as each has offered me a place in their home. That's a real twist from most children who would consider this a burden. At times it is enticing as my daughter and family live on an 80-acre farm in the rolling hills of Tennessee where the animals all live as part of the family and life is gentle and caring. My son lives on the high desert of southern California away from the big metropolis of Los Angeles. He is a library of knowledge from whom I have learned much. He has his doctorate in clinical psychology and must have proof before acceptance. I, on the other hand, have moved away from my technical orientation and receive most of my answers from intuition. We are different but that leads to great conversations and a respect for each other.

Part of me is a very social person and I have learned much from my association with other people. My service requires that I function in this real world. I am also a loner who desires much of the time in touch with nature and in communion with God. I am also a dreamer who lives in a fantasy land. That is mostly a secret part of me which seeps out only gradually. I constantly have visions of one world where there is peace and love, where we see each living thing as a soul, where we nurture each other in accordance with needs, expecting nothing in return.

If you see me on the street you may think of me as an ordinary senior citizen but, if you get to know me, I am a very complex person. I may seem to be one of the group, so as not to offend, but what is going on inside is a different story. I have always tended to be outside the mainstream but to be accepted as one of the in-group. I like to be the harmony rather than the tune. I always choose to play the counter-melody rather than the melody. I will always let you have your say then wait until tomorrow to have mine. Sometimes the meeting is over and my views were never known.

One thing I'm now realizing is that mostly what I have learned is from those who are part of the in-group, who generally agree with the message at hand, mostly getting views from like-minded people. So, I ask myself, should I spend more time listening to the dissenters marching outside the hall? Where is the right balance of all the voices? I see that I have a lot more to learn as my search continues... maybe from whole other segments of society.

Acceptance

Among the most gratifying changes that have occurred during my search include becoming more accepting and less judgmental. Very early in life I was told not to judge and to accept people as they are but I had very few role models to follow. Most of my elders, including my parents, teachers, and the church determined what was right and wrong and I began judging others by what I was taught. I learned who the sinners were and to avoid those that didn't fit my mold. I was continually trying to change others' behavior to conform to my own views of right or wrong.

In 1970 I was heavily involved in starting an emergency telephone service in Huntsville, Alabama. The most difficult aspect of the training was in teaching volunteer counselors not to judge callers but to accept them as people with problems needing help. We were compelled to learn *active* listening so as to avoid prejudging callers with our own hang-ups and programming. If a 14 year old girl called sobbing and afraid of telling her parents about her pregnancy, for many counselors their first reaction was "I have the answer". It was difficult to learn that our main response was to listen and be accepting of the caller without judging, and to project ourselves into their feelings. If the problem was serious we would refer them to our professional colleagues. I had to re-orient much of my own programming during this time.

At the same time I was teaching Parent Effectiveness Training courses to help resolve problems between parents and their children. The most difficult task was de-programming the parents and training them in more productive ways to change their children's behavior. The parents were determined to hold onto old learned habits. My experience has taught me that there are many skills we can learn to aid us in becoming more accepting and less judgmental but I find that as long as we operate from our five senses (the ego) we cannot avoid judgment at some level.

Many years later as my life began to change I had to deal with many issues that I could no longer justify. Even though intellectually I believed it wrong to judge another person I continued to find myself being critical of others' behavior, linking them to their behavior. As long as I live within these five senses it remains difficult to differentiate between the person and the behavior. If I operate from the spirit the more I can separate the two, and the better my chances of changing the behavior.

The more I am able to accept that life on this planet is the composite of all evolution and that our social mores are the result of our collective response to that evolution, the more I am able to accept that everything is exactly the way it is intended to be at any given time. An individual is a composite of genes, environment, social mores, and spiritual inputs, therefore, at any one instant that person reacts as a composite of all those inputs. If that person stops and thinks, or has outside influence, then he/she is not the same person and may react in a different manner.

Consider the following example. If I program a computer to perform a function and I provide certain data, the computer will give the same answer until I give it a different input. I must accept that answer and not judge the computer if it is not the answer I expect. I must accept the computer's answer until I reprogram it to give a different response. If the computer is broken then we repair it; if the response is not what we want we reprogram it. Although people are not computers, of course, the same principle hold true in that, at any given time, people respond in the same manner until they receive new input.

Understanding this principle allows me to be more accepting of the person and less judgmental of the response. If the person is broken we repair them. If the response is not the desired one then we reprogram the person. By this I mean that we must take some corrective action for improved social results but having this understanding allows me to respond in a more accepting and less judgmental way. As a result, not only do I have less stress and anger but I can be more objective in solving the problem. I must be certain that I have the right inputs. I look to God for those inputs.

In fact, this approach is not limited only to humans. It applies to all life on this planet. I have no right to judge what God has provided us through eons of evolution, therefore, I must accept every creature as responding to life with its present programming. Many years ago when I first watched nature shows on television and the tiger would chase and kill a zebra I would turn away as I could not bear to watch the suffering. Today, even though it is still a painful experience for me, I must accept that this is reality as intended.

I pray that I will continue to update my programming to new levels of thinking so that I may become more accepting and less judgmental of myself as well as others. Only then will I be more objective in my approach to solving problems and be more compassionate toward others.

Responsible Service

Many years ago while driving down I-65 to a road race in Mobile, Alabama, a new awareness came to me. As I was pulling out to pass a car in front of me I almost pulled into a car that was in the inside lane who was attempting to pass me. The car was in my blind spot. Even though I had checked my rearview and side mirrors I had not seen this approaching car. I assume each of you have been caught in similar situations. My first thought was to blame the other person for being in my blind spot, and then to blame myself for not being more watchful. For the next four hours my mind dwelled on "blind spots" and where my responsibility begins and ends.

Do I create blind spots for others and what is the connection between awareness and responsibility in such situations? Do we take advantage of another person's blind spots? In our personal relationships do we use this as a means of control or a way to put the other person down? At times do we intentionally let another person be the 'fall guy' to protect ourselves from blame? Legally there are specific laws that govern our relationships with others but does that relieve us of our moral responsibilities? How do I decide the moral issues?

To avoid responsibility we learn at an early age to blame

someone or something else when many times we are at fault. Soon it becomes a way of life. We have learned that telling the truth generally brings punishment. Most of us reach adulthood with the attitude that honesty does not pay. We carry this into our relationships and into our business life.

Since that day on my way to Mobile I have spent many years searching for a better understanding of the balance between awareness and responsibility. Today I firmly believe that all I become aware of carries an equal responsibility, not only to the other person but to myself. Some things I can only pray about, some things require personal action, and some things I must only pass on to some other source, but I must do something. As I become more aware of the crisis of our planet I can no longer sit on the sidelines. I have to take some positive steps toward the resolution.

When I come in contact with another person, animal, or any life, am I not now part of that life? If that contact comes through any of my six senses (the sixth being moral), then am I not morally, even if not legally, responsible to connect in some way? I must remember that there are always two or more views of every issue and I must be considerate of the needs and desires of all involved. If I can remember that everything in the universe is connected, I will approach each situation in a responsible way.

Recently, as I was riding my bike down a local street in Santa Cruz, I came upon a bike lock in the street. I chose to stop and pick it up. At that moment I became "locked" into that lock. What was I to do? After some thought I called the local paper and put an ad in the lost and found. I never received a response but I felt I had done the responsible thing.

In another instance, I found a purse on the beach as I went

for my morning walk. I took the risk of opening it, got the owner's address and returned it to a very happy woman. These are the things that most of us would do as honest citizens, but what about other situations that are far more subtle.

We all know about the bombing of the Federal Building in Oklahoma City that killed 168 people. It was devastating to me as it no doubt was to you. After the initial shock I asked myself what was the responsible thing for me to do. I had just become aware of a horrible catastrophe. It is not enough to pass it off and say, "I'm sorry but there is nothing I can do." As I was nearby, I could have driven to Oklahoma City and found some way to be of help to the survivors. As I traveled through Oklahoma City the next night it was pouring down rain and I just kept on driving! I continued my trip across the country but I could not forget the question: what was the responsible thing for me to do? Then I asked myself, how has my life been changed because of this incident? Through meditation I became aware that I have a powerful tool available that does not require physical action – *prayer*. I have prayed many times for all the survivors, leaving the results to God. That may seem trite but I did learn a lesson for myself. I really do believe that God can comfort and heal our pain, if only we prayerfully ask and let God provide the proper answer.

Many years ago, when our legal system was not so complicated we would bind agreements with a handshake. If I give you my word it is better than any legal paper you might have. Invariably, all legal documents can be contested and loopholes found. When I give you my word, there are no loopholes. I doubt today if ever a so-called legal problem is solved with a handshake. Our legal system assures us that nothing can be resolved without legal involvement.

As long as we have laws that govern our every move we become less apt to seek a moral solution. Many of our misfortunes could be resolved through arbitration if we educated arbitrators instead of lawyers. Our whole legal system is predicated on a win-lose result and many of the tactics are far removed from reaching a responsible settlement.

As I become more aware of the crisis of our planet I can no longer sit on the sidelines but have to take some positive steps toward its resolution. Devising a global solution is made more difficult because every country has its own set of values, customs, laws, and morals. We must be willing to accept the ways of other countries as we unite ourselves into one world.

As I continue my search for enlightenment I must constantly be aware of the impact that my actions have on others and the environment and make responsible decisions considerate of all life on earth.

The Elusive Soul

I feel that I have a reasonable concept of the mechanics of the body and even understand communications at the cellular level. With the use of the electron microscope we can get a look at the functions within cells. The problem is, that no matter how much we search, the soul does not appear on-screen, at least we have not recognized it yet.

As I conceive it, the soul is contained in the space within the cells and is not visible, weighs nothing, and contains no mass. Our present technology allows us to capture the smallest wave forms on screen (such as radio, microwave, and TV signals) but as yet has not been able to capture a soul wave. Is there such a thing? Is this energy in such a foreign form that our technology cannot decipher it? What is it in our bodies that detects this energy that can transform our whole being but yet cannot be detected? Maybe God has chosen not to give us the knowledge needed to understand this phenomenon at this time.

An atheist would claim there is no such soul signal to be found, an agnostic would question its existence until proven. The believer just accepts through faith and therefore don't get concerned over the process. Personally I know it exists and I believe, but my curiosity and engineering background want to understand the process. I'm not sure that all the mystics nor the great scholars of the past, or present, agree on the nature of this mystical reality. There is probably universal agreement that this point is deeply embedded in our psyche; however, the exact connection is a matter of interpretation. What is very clear is that those of us who have experienced this eternal love, even though fleeting at times, never question such divine intervention.

I believe that through meditation we can enter into the realm where we can fully transcend our bodies and enter into the universal spirit of love. There are times when I can break through all the layers of my physical being and bask in an outer source of beauty, tranquillity, and ecstasy. At other times I am totally in a space of human reality where I must deal with the material world with all its problems, along with its grandeur and beauty.

When we are young we tend to accept that our physical body is the channel to fulfill our purpose in this life. As we reach our middle years we begin to question what life is all about and search beyond materialistic goals to a more spiritual path. Many of us reach our later years and recognize that fame and fortune do not fulfill our hearts' desires; we are more comforted by spiritual matters.

Perhaps there is a natural transition where the soul is more attached to our young physical bodies and becomes more separated as we mature and age. At age 74 (chronologically speaking, of course), I find myself more detached from my body, seeking to be alone in nature and seeking guidance in pursuit of the *real Earle*. Probably, chronological age is not a big factor, but what this particular life has for us to learn is more dependent on our incarnation and our karma.

Another eye opener for me is the phenomenon of reincarnation and what happens to the soul when our physical bodies return to dust. What is the process for the soul to re-manifest itself into a new body? Years ago I didn't know what reincarnation meant, but after being in California for these past seven years, I find that most of my friends and spiritual teachers believe in reincarnation. My Christian background never dealt with this issue. As I am now open to learning about all spiritual teachings, reincarnation has appeal for me. In my continuing search I am open to become more enlightened on this matter and even open to becoming a true believer.

As part of my search I have been overwhelmed by the research available supporting the notion that the soul is universal and that we are all connected and become one when we can learn to communicate outside the complications of our own ego. It is very sad that most of us are never exposed to this body of knowledge. I became aware of this need for additional understanding of the soul as I searched deeper into my own spiritual life and found myself wanting.

In his book *Recovery of the Soul*, Larry Dossey reminds us that our Soul, Spirit, and Mind – separate from the mind associated with the brain – are truly separate from the Ego that we call our physical bodies. Dossey provides much research that we are all connected at a universal level. If we can learn to communicate at these levels, we can access great healing power that is unavailable through our accepted medical approach.

Occasionally, I will have some insight or intuition on this subject and think I have made a discovery only to find that much has been written by philosophers, physicists, scientists, and saints supporting the same insight that I have had. It lets me know that there is nothing new, only new to me. I marvel at the insight that comes to us from hundreds and thousands of years ago that is very relevant today.

Today I believe that the soul is the interface between the universal spirit and our physical bodies. As I become more open to the spiritual message, the soul interprets this awareness in a language that my intellect understands and transfers it to the right brain in the form of compassion and love. I shall continue seeking more guidance on the connection between the body and the soul. I believe wisdom does not come merely from an intellectual search, but from an open heart open to divine guidance.

Soul Mates

We are saturated with soul but few of us recognize it. At times we may get a glimpse but it flitters away. It is meshed with every cell, molecule, atom, and even our quarks, but still goes unnoticed. Occasionally we are aware of a glow in others who seem to be in some other dimension; but rather than join them we choose to continue to relate through our five ego senses.

I have wrestled with my soul most of my life trying to define and understand this nebulous part of me. When I was small I used to think it was my conscience. I can recall when I did something wrong and felt guilty, my conscience would hurt – a deep hurting in my throat. At times it was very painful. I believed if I was truly sorry and asked forgiveness the pain would slowly subside, but only if I were truly sorry. I wonder if others experience this condition today? By the time I reached my teens the pain had slowly diminished, and then disappeared never to be heard from again. Somehow, I had hardened my soul to where it didn't hurt any more. That was a relief, but on the other hand what was going to tell me when I had sinned?

A few days after writing a first draft of this chapter I was in the redwoods at early morning's light standing among the trees lost in my morning meditation. A vision of the people of the developing world would come across my mind with a horrible scene of death and starvation – tears rolled down my cheeks. Immediately I got an extreme pain in my throat, the same pain I had experienced 50 years ago as a child. And then I realized it was my conscience as I felt the social guilt that we all must share for allowing inhumane situations to exist on this fabulous planet of ours. All I was able to do at the time was to cry out, "God, why, why, why?"

In 25 years of active church life after the war, I still hadn't received answers on how the soul functioned. I was aware that God was in heaven and enters my body through my soul. Somehow the soul, being non-matter but housed in my heart, influenced the spiritual part of my life but had little impact on the intellectual left brain which guided most of my activities.

Ten years ago I stood on a street corner and watched a little old lady in her 80s slowly crossing the street. I watched, wondering what was going on inside this person. Why couldn't I touch her soul and know the great secrets stored there? Intellectually I knew she had feelings, desires, anxieties, hopes, and love, the same feelings we all experience. I was very frustrated because all I could see was a body which, for a fleeting moment, had come into my life and was now walking out of my life, probably forever. Had I lost some great wisdom that lay in store for me there? This was a great lesson for me.

Many evenings I have sat in the backyard and watched the planes pass overhead with their landing lights preparing to land at the San Francisco airport. I would picture about 200 people anxious to land and some wife or friend waiting for each of them. I would then pick out an individual on the plane, dressed up with a smiling face and I would talk to this person. I would hope they had a safe landing and that there would be a happy reunion upon their arrival. I would then wait for a response from that person that my message might have gotten through. I never got a verbal response but I am satisfied that my message did get through at some level.

Through the years this haunted me. I began trying to see inside the souls of other people. When I passed people on the street or pulled up beside them at a red light I would look at them and wonder if our souls might connect. Even though they did not respond and I was unaware if they felt a connection, there was a shift taking place within my own heart, and I truly believe that there was connection between our souls. I was becoming more compassionate toward others, more accepting of their behavior, and less judgmental of their actions.

I now believe that the only way to contact the soul of another is through meditation. It is not an intellectual choice and it is not through the service that I perform. If I can get in touch with my own soul then I am in touch with all other souls, and – even more astounding – I am also in touch with the universal soul. All these years I have been trying to contact the souls of others through my intellect. The wiser choice is through the spirit because that is the place where we are all connected.

I spent a recent weekend with my dear friends, Shams and Amanda. They have shared their spiritual experiences with me and my soul has been blessed with their acceptance of all religions and spiritual teachings. Often our themes concern the soul. We are able to see beyond the ego and connect in the spirit of pure love. They are surely my soul-mates. They also introduced me to a book by Pir Vilayat Inayat Khan, *The Call of the Dervish*. The Sufi Dervish provides a subtle presence in various forms that creates within us an Aha! or Eureka! which has transforming power towards true ecstasy. I am honored that I might follow in the path of a true Dervish and plant seeds of ecstasy wherever I travel.

Presently, I view the soul as the interface between God and my ego. As a new spiritual awareness comes to me through numerous channels, my soul gently massages my intellect (ego) nudging me to adjust, to be more compatible with the new spiritual message. Many times there is a battle between my left brain and my right brain before a conclusion is reached. If my right brain is the victor then a spiritual shift is made. If the left brain is dominant then I will ignore the new awareness and continue on my ego path.

As I am writing this chapter on the soul it happens to coincide with St. Valentine's Day so I shall take a moment to wish for you, wherever you are, a day of love and hugs. Take time out and tell someone you love them. Even though this day is primarily associated with romance, I hope you will consider this a move toward the deeper love we all strive for; the true essence of the soul, the universal love of God. I choose to take this as a day of fasting that further reminds me of that love, and to avoid all the chocolate bonbons. So, let us celebrate this day, as a day of love for all life on this earth.

I pray each day that I may become a more living part of my soul and that I may view all life on this planet as part of a universal soul. This allows me to see beyond the five senses into the spiritual world and accept all life as precious in the sight of God. As my search continues and I become more in touch with my own soul and if you are in touch with yours, then we will truly become soul-mates and be filled with joy because we will be in touch with each other and with the true essence of life. Will you be my soul-mate?

EGO-Mania

Our species has developed a collective and oversized ego, especially in the Western world. Not only do we as individuals have giant egos but so does our whole society, with the exception of the undeveloped nations, which are more concerned with survival. It seems we have become more self-centered and less caring about nature and the less fortunate. The difference between rich and poor continues to grow. Entrepreneur has become a household word and millionaires abound. Our ego seems to drive us to want more of everything and the more expensive, the better. While I am trying to down-size my own ego, the Western world seems to thrive on ego, growth, and expansion. The bigger the ego the less we seem able to solve the world's problems.

I am reminded of Maslow's Hierarchy Scale which is a guide from levels of safety and security to the self-actualized person, and I ponder where we are along this scale, and whether, at this point in history, are we able to become a self-actualized society. It seems to me that before we can escape our own ego body we must become self-actualized.

More and more of our technology and education allows us to feel that we are on the verge of knowing it all, that we are in charge. We can accomplish anything (except how to live in harmony with each other). When I was a young fellow there was a saying, "Young man, you're too big for your britches." That normally put me in my place. There has been a dramatic shift in the past 50 years from social values to technology and the computer has widened the gap. The computer age has allowed us to expand our knowledge to levels undreamed of a few decades ago. I am concerned that our ego is getting too big for our britches. After human cloning, what next? We are forced to decide social issues without the benefit of due process, and the pressure on our moral and spiritual values creates an upheaval in our emotional stability.

Computers allow us to put together unbelievable scenes that show up in movies, on the TV screen, and photos, where real subjects are a minor part of the action. We can put together the body of one person and the head of another and have it be undetected without expert analysis (as in the movie *Forrest Gump*). After the initial shock, we accept this as the way life is. Is there a moral question here?

When I sit under the redwood trees I ponder such things. What is going on in our world? Is there no stopping technology? Can we adjust to what is coming during the next decade? Am I using the redwoods as a place to hide? Will my own ego allow me to adjust or will I find excuses to sit back and wait until we destroy ourselves? What effort can I, as one individual, have on local and world affairs that can make a difference? If enough of us join together in a spiritual renewal we can help balance our ego with social needs.

As most of our daily activities are conducted through

our five senses, we need to keep searching for a well – balanced ego, one less threatening to our world. As we make tremendous breakthroughs in our technologies, what is going to keep us grounded? The newest computers can now make two million calculations in one second. Maybe one day soon someone will use the computer to figure out how much longer our species will last based on our present pace and direction. Our youth accept all this as routine. Look at our accomplishments in the medical field, in physics, in space, on the worldwide web, in every phase of human possibilities. Are we sure we are moving in a direction that is in balance with the universe? Is our course on self-destruct?

There is probably no way to stop our thirst for knowledge, but what can be done to make it beneficial for all life on the planet? Is it possible to use our wealth and our knowledge to the advantage of all the world's citizens? In school I learned that a good ego (self confidence) was needed to survive in the workplace and support my family. Today's ego is used to take advantage of every situation on a win-lose basis. The pronoun "we" has all but displaced "I, me, and mine." When we were all poor our ego was pretty well equalized. As we become more educated the "I" becomes more dominant.

It seems our technology is allowing us to bypass evolution, which, until the last century, necessitated us moving at a slower pace, being more in tune with nature. At least it could be 50/50 where we could ask ourselves: "Are we going in the right direction, considering the possible decimation of our planet and its inhabitants?" Being an engineer and part of the technical revolution, I can see the advantages which have come our way. I enjoy many of the benefits but I could be satisfied with a much simpler life. It surely is too late to turn back the clock, but we also need to put more emphasis on the right side of our brain so we may use this technology to our best collective advantage.

World Citizen

Intellectually, I consider myself a citizen of the world. Spiritually, I consider myself a citizen of the Universe. Legally, I am trapped in a system which says that my body has to belong someplace. I have not reached a space or time where I would want to denounce my American citizenship; that would complicate my life and the service that I have chosen. But in my mind and in my heart, I am a world citizen.

I continually ask myself how can I best fulfill my world citizenship. First, I must realize that whenever I wish, I can operate from a space where I can be in touch with all life at the same time, a place where no earthly laws apply. I have to do this from a totally different space than that in which my body operates. I have to learn a new (universal) language, one that comes from deep in the heart where all is connected. Some day I hope to physically travel the world but for now my biggest impact will have to come through internal communication and prayer.

When I was a young lad I could see no further than my immediate family, friends, and local community. World War II made drastic changes in the size of our planet. Even though the military might of our enemy was demolished, the humanitarian needs were overwhelming.

The war annihilated much of Europe and Japan but our collective conscience was willing to forgive in hopes of bringing world peace. We became heavily involved in the reconstruction of the devastation inflicted during a war that cost 60 million lives. During the years that followed, our country was acting as a world citizen when we reached a helping hand around the globe. During that period my world expanded from a little town in Tennessee to include countries I had never heard of.

During World War II there was no more patriotic person than myself, willing to die in the defense of my country. Today I am still very patriotic but my scope of country has changed considerably and includes all of the peoples of the planet. During our moon exploration, the views of the Earth showed no boundaries and I wondered why we should create dividing lines. During recent years I have been unable to limit myself within the boundaries of the USA. In this country our individual, state, and national politics protect our own lives, our boundaries, and our high materialistic standard of living. The *good book* tells us that we should treat everyone as our brother and love our enemies but our actions work to keep us divided. We have yet to learn that every life on this Earth is equally important to God. Undoubtedly we live in the most bountiful country in the world and we are blessed to live in the "land of the free." It is my prayer that we may share the fruits of this great land with all peoples of the Earth.

Because of the suffering and destruction of World War II, I became concerned about world problems and what keeps nations and peoples from living together in harmony. My concerns could no longer be contained to my own neighborhood. I recall the struggle of India to be free of British rule and the non-violent approach Gandhi used to accomplish this. His assassination was a great shock to me and to the world. Then followed the great invasion and take-over of Tibet by the Chinese, the Korean War, the Vietnam War, the assassination of Martin Luther King, the final collapse of Apartheid, the breakup of the Russian Empire, and the genocide that claims so many lives even today in so many lands. There continue to be so many global conflicts that cause tremendous misery. At times I am overwhelmed and wake up in the night with all the world's problems on my mind. I don't understand those who create these conditions but I have compassion for all who suffer under them.

I think of all the cultures that have been swallowed up by the export of the Western lifestyle. As the world shrinks and fills with more and more inhabitants, more cultures are lost forever. Is this what God had in mind when life began billions of years ago with the simplest of creatures in our oceans? As I wonder what one simple person (me) can do about all the ills of our society, I can only get on my knees and pray believing that God will intercede if we pray that "God's will be done" rather than "my will be done."

When the 1996 Olympics were in progress in Atlanta, I was overwhelmed watching the opening ceremonies as 197 countries, representing 17,000 athletes, paraded into the stadium. Even though they were competing against each other, there was only respect and honor in evidence. I have to admit I have some bias for the American individuals and teams, but deep inside I wish for all to be winners and I am just as thrilled when a person from another country wins a medal. When an individual reaches the highest reward in their field that person should have our praise regardless of nationality. As one who considers himself a world citizen I struggle with competition between countries, or even among ourselves. Our whole capitalistic system is based on competition but I find myself pulling for whomever is performing no matter which country they represent. I pray for the day when we not only love our neighbor but every living soul on our planet.

I suggest we have an Olympic event for all the politicians and heads of states around the world and let them mingle on a down-to-earth personal basis for a month. Rather than a sports event we could call it a peace marathon and offer medals for the winners of peace. The judges, of course, would not be politicians. Maybe some of our hate and fear would subside, and we could then build a world of trust, understanding, compassion, and equality for all. As the world leader (meaning most powerful) the USA must recognize that world peace is our most urgent goal. First we must tune the hearts of our own citizens to this cause.

There is always considerable news about human rights in the news. The State Department has recently issued its 20th annual report on Human Rights of 193 countries. These rights not only cover life-taking atrocities such as genocide but items such as women's rights, segregation, and child abuse. I am deeply affected by such atrocities and am proud of the accomplishments of the past few decades, but we must be extremely cautious how we approach these issues.

I can remember earlier this century when human rights were greatly flaunted and ignored in this country. We still have many internal trouble spots. We must recognize that much of the world is where we were 50-100 years ago and will not be bullied into complying with our standards. This country tries, in many ways, to force other countries into compliance with our standards. I much prefer this issue be resolved at the world level (United Nations) and through non-governmental organizations (NGOs) rather than through politics.

If I believe in the polls and what I hear and read from the media, most of us are willing to let the rest of the world gobble each other up while we protect our own borders and our own high material standard of life. Now that Russia is no longer a major threat to our country or the world, we are the outstanding super power on this planet and, as such, can wield a big stick to force our ways on the world. We must find a way to use our strength to improve the standards of all people on our planet. This can only be done through understanding, compassion, and acceptance of other cultures and views. It will never be attained through military might.

As I travel and mix with the public I always wear my badge of identification saying, "Earle – World Citizen". As I continue my search for the *real Earle,* world issues consume my thoughts and my service shall continue to move toward a helping hand that all might enjoy the wonders of our beautiful planet.

I trust that I might plant a few seeds that others might also begin to think like world citizens. If enough of us think that way then it will begin to happen, and we can become a truly great superpower. If you have concerns as I do for the future, spend some time each day in sincere reverence of this magnificent planet and all life on it.

A World in Crisis

Since my exposure during World War II, I have been concerned about what was happening on a world level. I have been considerate of the devastation and suffering of Europe and the Orient during and after the war and the reconstruction that followed, the founding of the United Nations to make the world a safer place for all peoples, the horrors of the 'Cold War', the numerous wars and destruction since, the suffering of the Third World, overpopulation, world hunger, and even the desperation of our own inner cities. Our world seems to be in continuous crisis. The more I search my own heart the more burden I feel to help resolve these conflicts.

Recently, while visiting my friend, Nelson Hellmuth, owner of the Granary Health Food Store in Orange Park, Florida, I was scanning some of the literature in his reading room. As I was about to leave Nelson picked up two books and said, "Take these along, they may interest you." The books are *Who Will Feed China*, and *State of the World*, both publications of the Worldwatch Institute. My friend had no idea about my interests in world affairs and, as I don't believe in coincidences, I knew this was more emphasis on a subject that concerns me.

For years I have read articles published by Worldwatch, but now, as I read in more depth about the problems we face on a worldwide basis, again I ask myself, "What do I do with this new knowledge?" I truly believe that God does not open doors until we have the capability to work with them, so I must spend my quiet time seeking answers to my newfound knowledge. I had stopped over at my daughter's for the holidays so I immediately read *Who Will Feed China* and was totally aghast by what I learned. This subject will be discussed in more detail in the chapter entitled World Hunger.

State of the World is updated yearly and gives the status of critical issues facing the world. It covers in depth such global issues as population, economics, fisheries, feeding the world, displaced persons, agriculture, groundwater, global warming, and many other crises that face us now and in the coming years. Each of these issues is potentially life-threatening for our species and must be dealt with from a global basis. When any country faces one of these crises then all other countries are affected.

When I was a kid what happened outside my own community was of little concern to me. Now, roughly 50 years later there is no place on earth that is not impacted by conditions in every other part of the world. Within the next decade or two we will know whether our species shall continue or become extinct. Will we join hands and support all the world organizations or will we continue on the path of self-destruction? The young people of today look to us for answers but thus far we are found wanting.

There are continuous crises throughout the world, but as the world grows smaller and the population grows larger, every crisis is magnified. As I am writing this chapter South Korea has had to borrow $57 billion dollars from the International Monetary Fund to avoid bankruptcy. A year ago this was unthinkable. Also, on the Pacific Rim the stock market is in great turmoil, with major repercussions for all world markets. World crises are having an economic impact on all of us, it cannot any longer be avoided. Overpopulation, malnutrition, the destruction of our food sources, the economic impact, and the whittling away at our environmental resources will impose a great threat to our ability to sustain life on this planet.

To cite an example of this sort of a crisis the world may soon face, consider China as it seeks to become a world superpower. Some of the issues that China faces today are overpopulation, human rights, industrial revolution, the inability to feed itself, low wages, student unrest, free press, possible economic disasters (such as the harnessing of the Yangtze River at a cost of $25 – $50 billion), and a lot of pressure from the outside world. As China struggles to become more democratic while under domination of Communist leadership, there will continue to be much unrest internally as well as externally from world pressure.

Whether China becomes an economic and human disaster for the world, as well as its own welfare, will depend on both how China copes with its own internal problems, and how the UN and other nations react to the internal affairs of China. After all, China has been in struggle for 5000 years, through many wars and dynasties, through occupation by many other countries, by religious and ethnic interference and by internal strife. It is not likely to be bullied by some 200-year-old country that has gone through many human rights problems of its own. We might consider China as backward and uneducated, with a controlled leadership that is doomed to failure, but we need to approach China with an open hand and an attitude of help rather than political and economic force. How we handle these issues can determine the outcome.

Now that Communist Russia has crumbled, China seems to be most capable of creating a major crisis on our planet; however, India and the Middle East are not far behind. Many African nations are in constant turmoil. In fact, very few countries aren't facing some crises as they struggle both within and without. We can no longer count on our political leaders to find a solution, so concerned persons and non-political organizations must offer a more compassionate approach for solving world crises. Political and military force is no longer capable of making the planet a better place to live for all peoples.

All I remember about China from my young years was that if you drilled a hole all the way through the earth from Tennessee you would hit China. I don't remember ever seeing a yellow-skinned person until I went into the Navy. We need to learn about China's history and its people and why the situation exists.

If you are interested in learning more about the history of China and their present dilemma I suggest you read *China Today* by Donald and Constance Shanor. Also, the September 1997 issue of *National Geographic* has an excellent article called *China's Three Gorges* on the nation's largest public works project since the Great Wall was built. This is concerned with harnessing 3000 miles of the Yangtze River.

Many years ago I taught classes on parent-child relationships. The first session was with the parents only. When I asked them why they were there the answer was, "I want to change my child's behavior." When I asked if the parents felt they needed to change their own behavior, from 0% to 10% answered yes. When I suggested that they might need to change their behavior as much or more than the child, I got a very cold reception. When I asked what expectations they had for their children when they finished school, their answers were all the right things, like I want them to be responsible, trustworthy, honest, obedient, unselfish, kind, happy, and all the nice things we all want. As the class progressed it soon became evident that the parents weren't very good role models; they wanted things from their kids that they weren't living up to themselves. In addition they had to learn how to communicate effectively with their children so the child didn't feel put down. If America wants to be a parent for all the world then we must live up to our own expectations, and learn how to communicate effectively with other countries with a genuine compassion for their culture, and their desires, and search for a win-win solution. Coming from a position of power supported by military might will only create more hate and resentment for this country and create more world tension.

I'm not an expert on any of the crises that are unfolding before us, but the deeper I search for the *real Earle*, the more I find these issues grieving my heart. If I consider myself a World Citizen and my mantra is service, what actions should I take to help heal the planet? As my search continues I look to the Universe to provide answers.

United Nations

As a World Citizen concerned with world affairs, I happened to be in California when the United Nations celebrated its 50th anniversary. The celebration actually started on April 22 to coincide with the 25th anniversary of Earth Day, and ended in San Francisco in early July with numerous dignitaries present including President Clinton. The long celebration allowed ample time to contemplate the achievements of the United Nations in its first 50 years.

Twenty-five years before the birth of the UN there was another noteworthy birth. The League of Nations was formed through the effort of President Woodrow Wilson after WWI to assure that a such a world conflict would never happen again. The President had most of the European nations in favor and spent time in Europe promoting the avoidance of another world war. He was greeted with great enthusiasm and was respected in Europe for kindling such an effort. However, President Wilson received so much flack from our own Congress that the US never supported the idea and the League of Nations gradually fizzled out in Europe.

Was such an organization simply before its time? Could it have prevented World War II? As I search my own soul for answers it is apparent that our collective conscience was just not mature enough to cope with the enormous problems of that day. I wonder if we are willing to pay the price even today to avoid another world war or even worse. Today the world is divided on the benefits of the United Nations, but what are our alternatives?

I have always been a supporter of the United Nations and its purpose. The greatest problem is that many of its member nations are dominated by those who cannot see beyond their own borders and stymie others who truly seek world peace and equality for all. When the UN was established its prime purpose was the security of the world so that people could live without fear. There was no understanding of the oncoming social, economic, and environmental problems at that time. Under most difficult circumstances the United Nations has performed admirably for 50 years.

But will the UN survive? It shall, but not through politics nor through power, but rather through a strong revival of the hearts of all people. When our collective (world) conscience reaches a critical mass (normally 20 – 25 percent) this will happen. I fully support the United Nations as a critical step in bringing about world justice and world peace. Without the UN where do we turn? Not that we all have to agree on all the issues, but we must view the world as our home, and all five and one half billion people as our family. If not, our whole species is at risk.

We have a tendency to be critical of the United Nations and forget its overwhelming accomplishments. It has been instrumental in keeping the peace, feeding the hungry, promoting human rights, ending Apartheid, improving children's lives, assisting refugees around the world, promoting women's rights, protecting the environment, and much more.

Presently Kofi Annan, the UN Secretary-General, has resolved the critical situation in Iraq. I heartily praise the Secretary-General for this resolution, and also praise the millions of prayers (including mine) that supported him in his mission of peace. I trust that this profound conclusion to the Iraq crisis will give greater credence to this most important World Organization.

A prime example of UN accomplishments was the Earth Summit held in Rio de Janeiro in 1992, formally entitled the Conference on Environment and Development. Most people probably don't even remember the event and surely not the continuing impact it has had on world affairs. Even I had to go back and review the impact of that summit. Almost all of the world environmental issues in process today emanated from the Earth Summit. There were over 100 heads of state that attended with their delegations, along with numerous Non-Governmental Organizations (NGOs) to sign agreements which promised massive impacts on the environment and development of the world.

I was so embarrassed that the last holdout to agree to sign the final document was the United States. At the very end of the summit there was so much pressure put on President Bush by environmental organizations that he consented, flew to Rio, and signed the document. I was so grieved by our government, not only as the leader of the free world, but the country that creates the most environmental damage on our planet. Though much has been accomplished as a result of the Rio Summit during the past five years, less than 50 percent of the signing countries have ratified the agreement and many of the programs are falling behind schedule due to politics, economics, education, and a lack of motivation.

I am saddened that politics around the world has derailed so much of the possible success in making our globe a more peaceful place to live. Even this country applies sufficient pressure to control much of the agenda. More recently the United States was instrumental in the ouster of Boutros Boutros-Ghali by withholding a billion dollars in owed back dues (which still hasn't been paid).

If you share my concerns for the future of our planet, spend some time each day in sincere reverence of this magnificent planet that is rapidly developing cancer. There is a definite correlation between the deadly diseases of the human body and the diseases of the planet. We desperately need a cure for the present condition, but also we need to apply prevention for the generations to come. We might heal both ourselves and the planet by applying the same methods: education, compassion, the elimination of greed, and prevention. The most damaging to both our own health and the health of the planet are toxins (both physical and mental). Our lifestyles leave behind enormous quantities of poisons with which neither the planet nor our bodies can cope.

I continually wonder why I am so concerned about world affairs. Why not leave it up to the UN and other World Organizations to solve such monstrous problems? Mostly, I have no choice. I care what happens to all life on this planet. I know the planet is also alive so I care about the planet itself. I care about the messes that we are leaving our children and grandchildren and all of those to come. And I care about the horrible things happening to most of the world, causing suffering beyond imagination. I can no longer limit my caring to family, friends, neighbors, local and national citizenship, to race, creed, religion, or color. To do so would be devastating to me as a human and spiritual being.

Recognizing my present physical limitations of being a

World Citizen, my mental and spiritual capacities do allow me to be any place at any time; therefore I can focus my energy and prayers on any spot on earth. In my search for the *real Earle* not only am I discovering my true service but also the spirit of the Universal God. Somehow, without the continued awareness that comes my way, I would probably be sitting on some fishing bank hoping for that big bass to strike.

 Finally, I want to introduce you to a person who only recently came into my life. His name is Dr. Robert Muller. He spent a 40-year career with the United Nations reaching the position of Assistant Secretary General. His focus was on world peace. He is now retired and is the Chancellor Emeritus of the University of Peace created by the United Nations. He was also a candidate for the UN Secretary-General in 1966, the post now held by Kofi Annan. Dr. Muller's awards and accomplishments are too numerous to mention here, but his latest book is a treasury of *Ideas and Dreams for a Better World,* a count-up of 2000 dreams to the year 2000. If you are interested in world peace this is a magnificent resource. For more information you may contact Dr. Muller and his wife, Barbara Gaughen Muller (also an author and educator), at Media 21, Santa Barbara, CA 93117, phone 805-968-8567, fax 805-968-5747.

 I support the United Nations as the most probable source at this time, to continue its many world programs to help bring peace to our planet. And I hope you will join me.

World Hunger

This is a fasting day for me and my thoughts naturally concern the abundance of food, or for a large part of the world, the lack of sufficient food. As I consider myself a citizen of the world I am continually confronted with the question of why we are allowing so many people to starve to death when we (collectively) grow enough grain to feed the world. To me it is a horrible crime against humanity, nature, and God for us to stand idly by and watch this cruel devastation while many of us in the Western World feast like kings and queens. Even though there are numerous worldwide organizations that are trying to solve this problem, it is only a fraction of what needs to be done, and *what could be done.*

If you are concerned with world hunger, *Who Will Feed China,* by Lester Brown, president of the Worldwatch Institute, is must reading. China's ability to feed itself is being seriously threatened by the combined impact of industrialization, population growth, loss of agricultural land, and water depletion. Unless things change drastically in the coming decades, China's need for imported grain could dramatically affect the world grain market, the environment, and the level of starvation.

China's ability to feed itself is not only a problem for China but for many of the developing nations. India's ability to support itself in the future follows the same path as China and will increase the economic burden on the world. This need for increased grain would also present a serious problem for the American lifestyle in the cost of living and the impact on the environment. I am concerned about my own grandchildren and all children of future generations. I wonder what kind of life is going to be there for them as we sit in the grandstands and watch.

As John Robbins points out in his book *Diet for a New America,* most of the grains produced in this country are fed to livestock. With a 10 percent decrease in meat consumption, Americans could free up enough land to grow grain to feed the starving people of the world. Of course, even if we did this that would not guarantee that the grain would reach the most needy. The hungry, after all, lack the economic and political power to secure adequate food. If this holds true in the future, as our population grows and industrialization shrinks the world's croplands, disaster lies ahead.

As a person who eats no meat, fish, chicken, or dairy products, I wonder why all of us can't reduce our meat consumption by 10 percent so that all may survive. Not only would this benefit the starving but we would be a healthier nation with less economic drain because of disease. But the problem will not be solved until we are willing to extend our concerns beyond our own boundaries to genuinely care what happens on a worldwide basis. I grew up in an environment where it was expected that 10 percent of our earnings be given to charity. Why can't we extend this to our food consumption?

While we are willing to spend our billions in search of a cure for cancer, AIDS, heart attacks, and other fatal diseases, we are unwilling to convert even a fraction of that to save starving children when there is already a known inexpensive cure – food. The irony is that we spend our billions seeking a cure for *preventable* diseases rather than focus on the cause, and essentially ignore this simple cure for starvation. The ratio of people starving versus people dying of diseases is far greater and the economic trade-off is disastrous. The cost of allowing one person to die of a major disease in this country could save the lives of thousands of starving people if we put the same emphasis on that effort. As I ponder this, it becomes more clear – we could easily do both if we had the political will to choose where we budget our billions of dollars.

The more I become aware of hunger and starvation against our own species the more I have to find personal answers for myself. Recognizing that the burden of resolution will fall on the shoulders of the few, I ask myself what I can do in trying to relieve this social menace called hunger. First, hopefully I can motivate you to take a personal interest in this world problem. Second, through my travels and speaking engagements, I may speak about this needless blight on our species. And thirdly, as I am able to put more of my energy and time on worldly problems, I may become more personally involved with some of the ongoing programs that desperately need our support. In recent months I have joined several existing groups trying to feed the hungry, and maybe you will do the same as a beginning to your own involvement. If you are on the World-Wide-Web you may search hundreds of possibilities where you can learn the magnitude of world hunger and the opportunities available to you for making a difference.

World affairs and world conditions have become a top priority for me as I determine the path of my service on this planet. First we must stop the killings and starvation that have become an accepted pattern of life. We must find new approaches to the ills of our world. Most of our energy and money are going into militaries and weaponry. So far that has led only to further destruction and economic ruin. World religions have failed to find adequate solutions to world problems and, in many instances, religious factions seem to promote hate instead of love.

I am thankful for all the world organizations that are providing a great service in combating disease and hunger throughout the world. But the answer will come more through prevention than healing. We tend to put power, profit, and greed at the forefront rather than prevention of wars, starvation, disease, and crime.

As I meditate on and contemplate this issue and seek my own involvement, in my frustration sometimes I ask God, "Why me? Who am I to take on the massive burden of world hunger?" And then I realize that this is part of the service path I have chosen, so I shall continue to educate myself and pray about world hunger and know, at some point, the handwriting on the wall will become clear. I do know that, as I search deeper into my own soul, my compassion for the starving and suffering of the world only intensifies.

Aging and Death

Our aging process begins at birth; we bring with it, through our genes, a certain amount of the evolutionary process. At this point our society takes control and, by the time we mature enough to make our own choices, the foundation is set. Early in life aging is hurried along as we learn to walk, talk, start school, reach our teens, finish school, get married, raise families, and send them out on their own. And then there is that long-awaited retirement. Unfortunately, by then, too many of us have lost our desire to live an enthusiastic productive life, giving way to chronic pains and illnesses, becoming dependent upon family or society, and slow death sets in. It is well-known that our organs are capable of functioning for over 120 healthy years. Even with all our medical technology the average person in this country will die a painful death by age 75.

Even though I am reaching that magic age of 75, I believe I have wiggled out of this social trap (mostly) and my view of aging and death is not a deterrent to my living. Of course, as long as my body allows me to be of service to God and the planet I want to prolong death until my karma is played out in this round. My only request is to choose the day and the way I leave this old ego form behind. Even though I have been exposed to reincarnation, in recent years I do not think it plays a part in the quality of my aging process. Even though it might be comforting to know that I may return to continue my universal aging process at another time, I am not too concerned during this round as I am too involved in searching for the *real Earle* and, of course, serving humanity and God.

Much has been written about aging and death. As you know, death is one of our biggest fears. We are taught from birth to avoid death at all costs but soon enough it catches up with us. It is not when we die that matters but how we die. Many have died heroic deaths, some have died violently, some by choice, some painfully, some as martyrs, and the list goes on. Aging and death are critical issues for our society and we must begin to deal with these issues, or they will be the death of us all!

New technology, medical advances, and health improvements have helped increase our life span 50 percent just in this century. My parents both died at age 53 and they were considered "middle-aged" with their best years behind them. Today, at 74, I still feel in my prime. I expect to live a healthy, productive, non-dependent 100+ years. Then I'll decide what to do with the rest of my life. When I think of my goals, I envision myself one day being the oldest living World War II veteran. Why not? I was 17 when I joined the Navy and I suspect that half of the 15 million veterans have already passed on. Further, I'm probably in better shape than 99+ percent of the remaining veterans. If you are a WWII veteran you may want to challenge me. Maybe we could start a club.

I always see myself as the same age of those I am associating with. If you are 40, then I mirror myself as being 40. If you are a teenager then so am I. However, 50 is my limit. Young people have always been an important association of mine and encourage me to keep a youthful attitude and to think young.

A few years ago I went to my 50th high school reunion. I had not seen most of these people in 50 years. I guess I was expecting to see people as young as me (!) but what I saw was a different story. You see, from my eyes, I was seeing all those classmates as young as I was viewing myself, and as young as when I had last seen them. Except for Jimmy Eanes, who I don't believe has aged a day since high school, I was shocked as he looked as young as when he graduated. This reunion has reminded me to continue seeking ways to age gracefully and enjoy my senior years.

Our youth-fixated society has completely failed to help us view aging and death as a process to be nurtured and accepted as a natural part of life, one to be enjoyed to the fullest until the day we shed this burdensome form and enter into life eternal, or prepare for our next return. Even though we have increased our life span to the middle seventies, many of us live miserable lives in our supposed "golden" years, as we feel we are outcasts from the mainstream of life. Many older cultures view aging with wisdom, respect, and honor. In this country we have degraded our seniors with a "put out to pasture" mindset that leaves us without hope for productive years.

Retirement has become a dividing line between productive and non-productive years. The last year before I left the government to join the ranks of the unemployed (I detest the word retirement) I had a large calendar on my wall. I would cross out each day with a big red X and each day I would ask myself, "Earle, are you sure you will see yourself as important after you leave this job? If not, don't leave." I had to be sure that my self-worth would not degrade as I shifted my emphasis in life. Twelve years later I can truthfully say that my self-image and self-worth have far exceeded my expectations. I believe the single most important factor in this transition is what we think of ourselves. Find something productive to do to ensure that your life has meaning.

During my working years I used to dream about how I would occupy myself when I reached that magic age. At one time I thought I would retire to the farm and hunt and fish. At other times I thought I might become a minister and have a little country church. Or perhaps I would start a community center for the economically depressed. All of that changed as God had other plans for me. My present plans are to travel the earth with a message of health, hope, and peace, planting seeds that others may also prepare for productive lives, not only through their middle years, but as seniors and even until death.

Some people hate their age to be known, even in their 30s. I am excited to tell the world that I'm 74 and looking forward to 75 then 80 then 100. Actually, I think I have more credibility the older I get. I get so much positive feedback from my friends and when I'm on the road speaking to groups, the questions are more related to my personal story than the message I bring. I know that the messenger is not as important as the message but it does boost my ego.

Ram Dass, one of my spiritual mentors, is an excellent resource on the subject of aging. From him I have learned both how to live and how to die. It is with great sadness that I learned recently that Ram Dass suffered a stroke that left his body in great distress. However, he is recovering sufficiently to help in the final phases of his latest book on aging, and to be with us physically with his great wisdom as he continues to be with us spiritually. It is very difficult for me and his followers to understand why this western Guru – who has been a spiritual leader to the multitudes – has to endure this great tragedy. As with many of our great leaders, tragedy seems to come far too early in their imprint upon this planet.

Many of our great masters have died early in life, many with serious illnesses. It is not a matter of how long we live, it is the quality of life that determines our worthiness as mortals on the earth. When I reach the point that my life can no longer be productive, when I am taking more than I am giving, then I will be ready to be with the angels and archangels (I hope) awaiting further instructions.

The greatest death story I know is that of Scott Nearing as paraphrased from his wife Helen's book, *Loving and Leaving the Good Life*. Several months before Scott's 100th birthday he began to slow down his activities on the farm and began planning for his future life. He and Helen had a long and beautiful life together and their lives have left a beautiful legacy for all of us to share. Scott, realizing that his productivity was gradually coming to an end, one day said to Helen, "I think I'll only have juice." She respected his request and gave him only juice. As he approached his 100th birthday he said to Helen, "only water, please" and, out of her great love for him, she did as he wished. A short time later, now confined to his bed, he said, "no more water, please." She knew what this meant and understanding his desires, followed his wishes. In a short time, while holding Helen's hand, he passed on. Scott, in no pain, slipped away to another life. What a marvelous story! I pray for the courage to accept death as Scott did and thus choose the way and the time that my life on earth shall end.

As I continue my search for the *real Earle* I look forward to more awareness on the full understanding of the importance of life, aging, and death. I pray that you will avail yourself of the many powerful books on aging and dying to avoid having to confront this issue unprepared in your declining years.

The Future Search

The more I learn about my inner self the more doors are opened. The more I become aware and the more God's truth is unveiled, the more I realize that the search is endless. The search will end only when I shed this form called "me" and become totally spirit. Even then my spirit will continue to live as part of the great universe of love, awaiting my next assignment.

Somehow, as this search continues, I must share both an ego trip and a spiritual journey. It is beyond my comprehension why evolution has developed this burdensome physical form that has entrapped the sweet essence of the divine; however, for now I must accept this reality and be thankful for the opportunity and the challenge to make the transition from one state to another.

Though my life has always been one of service, I must continue to search for balance between the spiritual and the physical and the interrelationship between the two. The more I meditate and become aware of the spirit the more I am consumed with the joy and serenity I feel. I don't see myself becoming a monk but I must say that the more quiet time I spend with God the greater the temptation there is to forget earthly matters. On the other hand, there is much to be done to help others find joy and peace in a world of chaos where many are still in survival mode.

As the search continues there will be many choices to make. In my past I have set goals and watched many of them become reality. In the future I shall set fewer goals knowing that the process is more important than the goal itself. The more I remove myself from the results the more rewarding will be the process. Also in the future I shall continue to screen my life of material clutter that saturates my five senses, and open more doors to the senses beyond.

Even though I have been searching for the *real Earle* for many years, the past eight years have been an upward spiral, especially in my search for infinite love. I recognize that each step I have taken throughout my life has been important in reaching my present plateau, but in recent years the process has been phenomenal. My arrival in California was a drastic change in environment, especially in my spiritual development. There seems to be no end to the variety of paths to choose from as spiritual leaders abound. Now as I travel around the country I carry with me much of the California lifestyle that has enriched my life. I also have found that it is not important where I am as my search is contained primarily within myself. However, I continue to learn through the wisdom of others, from nature, and from all life on the planet.

I will consider my search ended when I have been transformed from the somebody state (ego) to the nobody state (awareness). My search will end as I physically slip out of this form and my spirit again ripples throughout the universe awaiting its next assignment. My journey may not be complete, and may not be for many eons to come, but I will know that I have raised my own consciousness on this earth, getting a glimpse of eternity.

I trust that you too are on a similar journey and that we may someday meet and share our journeys together.

Forever Joy, Peace, and Love Amen!

How to Contact the Author

When I retired in 1985 I chose to never accept personal financial gain for any endeavor for the rest of my life. Instead, I have chosen a simple lifestyle of volunteering my services and donating any monetary gain to worthy organizations promoting the welfare of our own health, the health of the planet, and most of all, the health of our spirit.

If you would like me to come and speak to your group about my experiences or to order my book, you may contact me by e-mail: peasamb@aol.com, write to me at P.O. Box 2174, Santa Cruz, CA 95063, or leave a message on my voice mail, (831) 427-4567.

110 *The Search for the Real Earle*

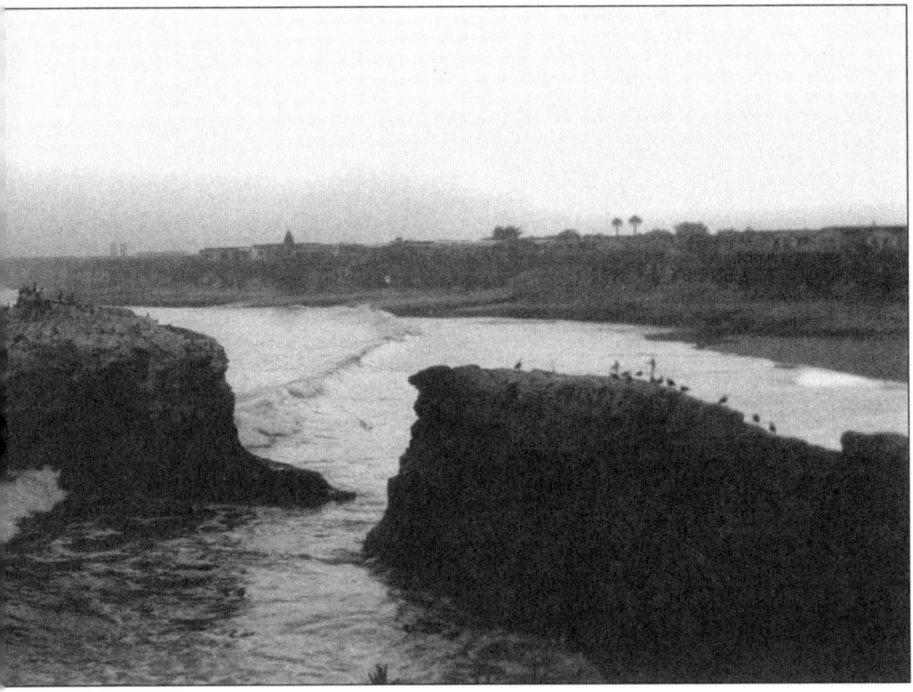

112 *The Search for the Real Earle*

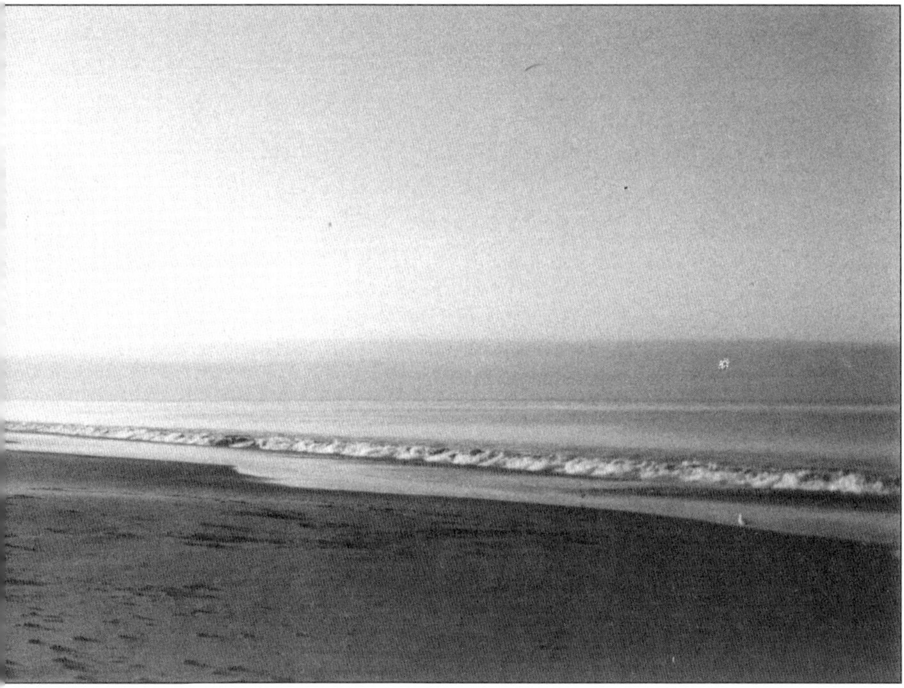

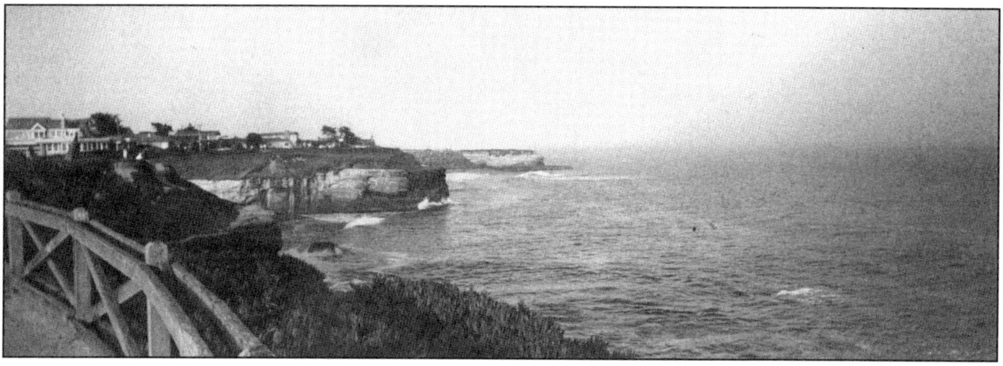

Order Form

Please send me _____ copy(s) of *The Search for the Real Earle*. I understand that I may return any books for a full refund.

_____
NAME

_____
COMPANY NAME

_____
ADDRESS

_____
CITY   STATE   ZIP

_____
TELEPHONE

e-mail: peasamb@aol.com
Price: USA $9.00 each book, Canada $12.00 each book.
Shipping: $3.00 first book, $2.00 each additional book.
Payment: By check or money order only.
Send orders to: **True Heart Publishers**, P.O. Box 2174, Santa Cruz, CA 95063 (831) 427-4567